T0248034

how we channel our resilience and perseverance, and how we overcome! This is a book for everyone invested in ensuring the next generation of great companies is launched by the best variety of individuals our world has to offer.

—COCO BROWN
Founder and CEO of Athena Alliance; 100 Most Powerful People of Silicon Valley

This book illustrates what is possible when you build a culture of inclusion, where the best ideas can open new and adjacent markets or create value. Great leaders support innovation from all areas of the company and empower women at all levels to be seen, valued, and heard. I was fortunate to partner with Kelley along her entrepreneurial journey when I was the CEO of HERE Technologies and to share her vision for the future of work. Kelley's message in the book is clear— the world will benefit from more female intrapreneurs and entrepreneurs disrupting the status quo.

—EDZARD OVERBEEK
Former CEO of HERE Technologies and Board Director of KPN and CVC

Valley Girls represents the core philosophy Kelley has lived in her professional life. I have had the privilege of being a part of her journey from CHRO to entrepreneur and seeing firsthand how she took many of the concepts as a thought leader in the future of work and applied them to her own career. In these pages, she has an inspirational message to female innovators to live a growth mindset, go after their dreams, and to pursue each of their entrepreneurial paths with eyes wide open.

—JOHN BOUDREAU, PHD

Professor Emeritus and Senior Research Scientist, University of Southern California, Author of *Reinventing Jobs*, *Lead the Work*, *Work without Jobs*, and *Investing in People*

Valley Girls is a must-read for all aspiring entrepreneurs and investors, regardless of their gender. Kelley Steven-Waiss builds upon her eye-opening personal experience with incredible stories of women who have achieved success by embracing their own strengths and lifting others up instead of conforming to the stereotype of the hard-charging disruptor that has been historically glorified in Silicon Valley. *Valley Girls* provides a much-needed expanded blueprint for how it looks to change the world with technology and will surely inspire a new generation of collaborative leaders.

—ALLISON BAUM GATES

General Partner, SemperVirens, and Author of *Breaking into Venture*

Valley Girls is an empowering beacon for aspiring women entrepreneurs. With invaluable insights, strategies, and stories from successful trailblazers, this book invites all of us to rewrite the rules and create meaningful impact together.

Kelley's experience is inspiring as a road map for entrepreneurial dreams to become a reality.

—EVA SAGE-GAVIN
Senior Managing Director, Talent and Human Potential at Accenture

The proverbial climb to the top can be a lonely one. In her book, Kelley Steven-Waiss pulls back the curtain to reveal a sisterhood of successful women who candidly share the setbacks and triumphs of their journeys, showcasing that with hard work, passion, and perseverance, everyone can achieve extraordinary things. A great reminder that, as leaders, we should act with an abundance versus scarcity mindset, celebrate the wins of those around us, and champion the next generation in order to achieve a world of equality, opportunity, and diversity.

—KIRSTEN RHODES
San Francisco Managing Principal, Deloitte LLP

In *Valley Girls*, Kelley Steven-Waiss has captured vivid snapshots of the undeniable contributions of Silicon Valley's iconic women entrepreneurs. Her own tremendous accomplishments provide her with a unique lens for illustrating the untold story of the women founders who helped shape technology's landscape of innovation.

—GARY A. BOLLES
Author of *The Next Rules of Work* and Chair for the Future of Work for Singularity University

The "start-up founder's journey" has been well documented in many strong-selling books yet almost exclusively from the male perspective. In a world where women continue to break barriers, *Valley Girls* offers us a view of that journey from the female perspective. This book is an indispensable resource, empowering women to embrace their unique capabilities to tackle the opportunities and risks founders face. A must-read for every woman ready to make her mark as an entrepreneur.

—ANGEL MENDEZ
Former COO of HERE Technologies, Chairman of LevaData, Board Director of Kinaxis, Peloton Interactive, Sleep Number Corporation, P33 Chicago

In my almost fifty years of building the Radford Survey business, I have had the opportunity to meet and work with many very talented women. They are a large part of why Silicon Valley is so successful and important to our world. Kelley Steven-Waiss has the unique perspective by operating at the highest level in the organization as a CHRO and founding a company which was acquired by Service Now. I dare say there is no one else who could have written a book like this about the experience of female founders in the Silicon Valley.

—JOHN RADFORD
Founder of the Radford Surveys

Valley Girls: Lessons from Female Founders in the Silicon Valley and Beyond is a beacon of inspiration for aspiring women entrepreneurs, offering a road map to triumph against all odds. *Valley Girls* is not just a story of resilience but also a call to action for women to break barriers, challenge norms, and carve a space for themselves in the entrepreneurial world. Kelley's captivating and insightful book serves as a guiding light, reminding us that when women with big ideas step into the arena, they pave the way for progress, innovation, and a more inclusive tomorrow. *Valley Girls* is a must-read for anyone seeking to make a difference, proving that when women dare to dream, they can achieve the extraordinary.

—AMY CAPPELLANTI-WOLF

Former CHRO of Cohesity, Board Director of BetterWorks, D-Wave, Wellist

Good leaders provide direction, purpose, and reason for a group or organization to follow. They also share their knowledge, wisdom, and experience with others. Their leadership becomes a calling to serve others. Kelley Steven-Waiss is a leader who generously shares her wisdom in *Valley Girls*—a fun read and totally on target for today's business and social climate.

—JENNY DEARBORN

CXO Operator, Board Director, Angel Investor, Former CHRO, Author of *Data-Driven Leader*

I've had the honor and pleasure of working for women at almost every level—from management, to CEO, to founder. Kelley Steven-Waiss has always been a leader in our profession. And she's one part of a long history of powerful women who drove change to impact climate, built companies from zero to hero, and tackled the significant challenge of equal opportunity for

America's workforce. I am so grateful for the inspiring women in *Valley Girls* who paved paths, dispelled myths, and busted stereotypes so that my daughter and so many other young women can continue to carry the torch forward. Thank you, Kelley, for bringing these important and compelling stories to light.

—DEAN CARTER
CHRO, Fossil, Patagonia, Guild Education

That old saying "it takes one to know one" can be applied here. The author, a success story in her own right, knows that nothing much happens without struggle. She knows the treacherous path, the dangerous path, and the sweet path of getting there. That's why these chapters and the lessons in them will stick for a long time.

—DR. BEVERLY KAYE
Author, Thought Leader, and Keynote Speaker

Realistic while at the same time inspiring! *Valley Girls* provides a candid look at the bias that exists and what it takes to succeed as a female entrepreneur by sharing lessons and hard-learned wisdom from some of the most visionary leaders in the Silicon Valley today. Waiss provides a thoughtful reminder of the value of an abundance mindset over a scarcity mindset—a lesson that applies not only to entrepreneurs but also to people in all phases of their career and life journey. Worth the read!

—DAWN ZIER
Former CEO of Nutrisystem and Chair of the Hain Celestial Group

VALLEY
Girls

:// **KELLEY STEVEN-WAISS**
[FOREWORD BY ADRIANA GASCOIGNE]

VALLEY Girls

[
LESSONS FROM
Female Founders
IN THE
Silicon Valley
AND BEYOND
]

Forbes | Books

Published by Forbes Books, Charleston, South Carolina.
An imprint of Advantage Media Group.

Forbes Books is a registered trademark, and the Forbes Books colophon is a trademark of Forbes Media, LLC.

Printed in the United States of America.

10 9 8 7 6 5 4 3 2 1

ISBN: 979-8-88750-217-5 (Hardcover)
ISBN: 979-8-88750-218-2 (eBook)

Library of Congress Control Number: 2023919119

Book design by Analisa Smith.

This custom publication is intended to provide accurate information and the opinions of the author in regard to the subject matter covered. It is sold with the understanding that the publisher, Forbes Books, is not engaged in rendering legal, financial, or professional services of any kind. If legal advice or other expert assistance is required, the reader is advised to seek the services of a competent professional.

Since 1917, Forbes has remained steadfast in its mission to serve as the defining voice of entrepreneurial capitalism. Forbes Books, launched in 2016 through a partnership with Advantage Media, furthers that aim by helping business and thought leaders bring their stories, passion, and knowledge to the forefront in custom books. Opinions expressed by Forbes Books authors are their own. To be considered for publication, please visit books.Forbes.com.

In honor of my beautiful and passionate daughters, Maddie and Ella.

May you always follow your dreams and never be held back by any limiting beliefs. You can achieve anything you set your mind to.

Contents

Myths of Successful Founders

Taking Flight

Moments of Truth

Organizational Antibodies and the Swim Upstream

Inside Out

Acknowledgments

I could not have written this book without the support of my husband, Vincent; my four children (Jack, Griffin, Madison, and Ella); and my amazing ServiceNow colleagues, mentors, and friends. You listened endlessly to my ideas, read draft chapters, and offered your invaluable perspective and feedback. I feel blessed to have you all in my life.

I wanted to thank the amazing female founders who I had the privilege to get to know over the course of writing this book. Not only did I enjoy our conversations over coffee, lunches, dinners, and Zoom calls, but I also learned so much from all of you. I realized that my entrepreneurial journey through challenges and triumphs was not unique to me, that we shared so many experiences that only female founders could know or understand. In so many ways, writing this book was therapeutic. It was exhilarating to hear your stories and share these experiences with one another. Many of you have become friends, and the coffees, lunches, and stories will continue.

I want to thank my lead investors Bill and Will Elmore for taking a leap of faith on Hitch as an early-stage start-up backed by a female first-time founder. I appreciated your guidance and support. I want to thank the Broadway Angels—M.J. Elmore, Catherine August

DeWilde, Carla Newell, and some of the amazing early LPs (Limited Partners) from How Women Invest (too many to name here) as well as Bluestem Capital, Tyler Stowater, and Drew Doshier. I especially want to thank Judy O'Brien who not only invested her money but also her guidance and coaching along the length of this journey. You are like a big sister to me, and you were my rock!

I want to thank my good friend and former colleague Brian Lent, a serial entrepreneur and great human being, for listening to my big dreams early on when we worked together at HERE Technologies and for always being there for me behind the scenes to coach, counsel, and let me vent as one founder to another.

I want to thank my former boss and CEO of HERE Technologies, Edzard Overbeek, for allowing me to follow my passion, which led to the successful launch of Hitch. I learned so much from you. And, to my HERE colleagues who were pioneers of a new technology and who opened their hearts and minds to a new way of working. I especially want to thank my Hitch colleagues (past and present) for believing in the dream and putting in the time, passion, and energy to make it a reality.

I wanted to thank the team at Forbes Books for the teamwork and collaboration, especially Diana Holquist and Lauren Steffes. I appreciated your level of professionalism and support in managing every aspect of the publishing and editorial process. You have been amazing partners!

ACKNOWLEDGMENTS

With special thanks:

Kelly Ryan Bailey

Allison Baum Gates

Mackenzie Branigan

Denise Brouder

Maria Colacurcio

Barbara Fagan

Adriana Gascoigne

Kathryn Hanson

Denise Hummel Isaacson

Dr. Beverly Kaye

Jody Madala

Deidre Packnad

Nancy Pfund

Ashley Reid

Miriam Rivera

Sheila Talton

Sally Thornton

Janine Yancey

Foreword

You may be wondering why I chose to write the foreword for *Valley Girls*. Beyond Kelley and I both being founders and growing up in the San Fernando Valley (Southern California), we also were exposed to a family of entrepreneurs and had mothers who acted as strong female role models. There was something about that shared experience of humble beginnings, scrappy parents, and our pursuit of an entrepreneurial path with a good dose of fearlessness that made us bond immediately.

Stepping into the entrepreneur's journey is not an easy one and can be filled with a lot of emotional and physical toil. When you hear about the pixie dust of the Silicon Valley, somehow the realities of what it takes to succeed get lost in translation. Not every founder has a fairytale-like experience that lands in a huge exit or initial public offering (IPO), and often the journey to get your business off the ground has several twists and turns. To date, no one has told the story from the female founders' perspective quite like this.

From my own experience in technology and then founding an organization called Girls in Tech to support our future female leaders, I experienced many of the things that you will learn in the pages of this book. I know that it takes a balance of risk and confidence, being focused on your mission and yet open-minded, taking smart risks and having faith in yourself, and being resilient when you face inevitable rejections and disappointment.

You see, my mother was an immigrant. She woke up every day with a burning desire to succeed and appreciated her freedom to have choices. She saw obstacles as inconvenient but not insurmountable. I learned very early on that you could be anything you dreamed of, but you would have to work hard for it.

What I didn't know then or didn't realize was that the path as a female entrepreneur would be marked by ups and downs and shaped largely by the way I would experience that the world wasn't going to welcome me with the same passion and energy I brought to it—my resilience and resolve would be tested numerous times. Looking back, I know that my ability to persevere and become successful was how much the "village" of people around me or "my tribe" is what helped me navigate those rough waters.

When I think about what really made me want to become an entrepreneur myself, I believe that it was this deep belief in myself (thanks to my parents) and that anyone could have an impact, including me. I went to college at UC Davis, and after graduating in 2000, I got my first job in an advertising and PR role with Hill & Knowlton. My passion for social issues led me to work on campaigns for CA Governor Gray Davis, such as "No Smoking," "Partnership for Responsible Parenting," and "Healthy Families." I realized how much I succeeded when I was working on something I was passionate about. It was also then that I got my first lesson in leadership.

I was working for a Latina boss. I figured we both spoke Spanish, and we would bond like sisters. Shortly, I realized that she didn't share my enthusiasm for her work. She found my youthful, energetic attitude patronizing, and she threw cold water on every idea I brought to the table. She didn't support me at all, and I found that really demotivating. *Weren't all women, especially, those who share a cultural bond, going to have the same effect?* It was after that experience that I told myself I would never lead with anything but care and compassion. I would honor the girl who speaks up and leads from her heart. It turns out, that experience was, in large part, the genesis of Girls in Tech.

> Our world needs women to speak up, share their ideas, and to be heard.

Today, I am fortunate to lead a nonprofit organization dedicated to building the next generation of female leaders and the next generation of female technology entrepreneurs who will change the world in some profound way. Girls in Tech is dedicated to eliminating the gender gap in technology, and today we have over 110,000 members and exist in fifty cities around the globe. I believe strongly that every girl needs to be heard and that with inclusivity, we build a better world. Our world needs women to speak up, to share their ideas, and to be heard.

I hope that as you read this book, you see yourself in some of these other women's stories like I did and that you find a way to encourage women to speak up and to share their ideas with the world. I know we can only change the world for the next generation of "Valley Girls" if we find a way to lift one another up and show the way forward.

Adriana Gascoigne
FOUNDER AND CEO, GIRLS IN TECH

Introduction

> Everything I've achieved has come from perseverance. I've never met another entrepreneur who had a painless path to success—everyone who tries to bring new ideas to the world is tested. All aspiring entrepreneurs should remember that failure doesn't mean the end of the road. It can lay the groundwork for something even greater.
>
> **—RASHEMA SAUJANI, FOUNDER, GIRLS WHO CODE**

You have a great idea that can change the world, or at least a small, important part of it. You can't sleep without dreaming of it. You can't wake without it being on your mind. Come hell or high water, you are going to make it happen.

But if you're a woman smart enough to have that kind of big idea, you're also smart enough to understand that the odds are stacked against you. In 2021, 2 percent of venture capital funding went to companies with female-only founders, the lowest percentage since 2016.[1] Women seeking capital run up against negative stereotypes,

---

1   Pitchbook, "US VC: Female founders dashboard," February 1, 2023, https://pitchbook.com/news/articles/the-vc-female-founders-dashboard.

cultural biases, sexual harassment, and discrimination—even from other women. To make matters worse, the focus on a few heralded success stories and the perception that women have an advantage because of entitlements have created the illusion of progress where little exists.

And yet, there is a path forward for any woman with a great idea and the passion to succeed. I ought to know. July 1, 2020, my SaaS tech company, Hitch Works, became a female-founded, venture-backed company. It was one of the most exhilarating days of my life. I still get emotional thinking about it. It took years of work and sacrifice to navigate that vast chasm between idea and reality. I've been a chief human resources manager (CHRO), chief innovation officer (CIO), and chief executive officer (CEO), but founding Hitch was the hardest thing I've ever achieved. I had decades of experience at every level on the corporate ladder, but I still had so much to learn about entrepreneurship and the treacherous world of venture capital. I wished that I had a guide along the way.

I wrote this book to be *your* guide. I spoke to dozens of female founders who also succeeded despite the odds. What did we all have in common? Which strategies brought success, and which failed spectacularly? I wanted to pull back the curtain to reveal everything from our heartbreaking setbacks to our exhilarating triumphs.

Each founder's story provides a guiding light for a different stage of the entrepreneurial journey. How exactly did CEO and founder Sally Thornton get her idea for Forshay off the ground? How did CEO and founder Sheila Talton craft her pitch and choose her targets to build Gray Matter Analytics into what it is today? What made CEO and Founder Ashley Reid succeed at scaling where others before—and after—her failed? And why did founder and CEO Denise Hummel

Isaacson, J.D., sometimes decide to take the intrapreneurial and other times the entrepreneurial path?

I spoke to women in diverse industries, from nonprofits to consumer products to tech. I talked with women of all ages, from their thirties to their seventies. I tapped female founders of different ethnicities, nationalities, races, religions, and abilities to ensure that every reader could find themselves in these pages.

After hours of conversation and analysis, several conclusions emerged. The first and most important is that if we did it, you can, too. We were ordinary women who achieved extraordinary things with hard work, grit, passion, and perseverance.

The second is that

> When women succeed, they inspire an atmosphere that opens doors not just for other women but also for everyone who benefits from a more inclusive and supportive workplace environment.

there's a sea-change underway, and you can be a part of it. Women are winning. We're getting there. I see it when I turn on the news and another female police chief is commanding the podium. I see it at conferences when a female CEO delivers her brilliant keynote to an audience composed equally of male and female C-suite executives. I see it in the stories of these female founders. And I see it when a male venture capitalist writes me a check because he believes not just in me but also in the world he and I are helping to create together for his daughters.

We also found that female founders make a difference. The stories in these pages show that there is something fundamentally different about how successful women operate in the business world. Collaboration, consensus-building, and a deep sense of purpose are hallmarks of successful female founders. This is important for everyone, because when women succeed, they inspire an atmosphere that opens doors not just for other women but also for everyone who benefits from a more inclusive and supportive workplace environment.

And yet, not all our findings were positive. A constant theme I heard in my research was that too many women aren't reaching back to help the next woman succeed. For every step forward, we're taking ourselves two steps back. We abandon our superpowers, the very characteristics that made us successful in the first place, because once we reach our goals, a scarcity mindset takes hold. A voice born of insecurity and fear tells us that there's only room for one seat for a woman at the table. We must understand why sometimes women act this way and then act differently.

The female founders in these pages did just that. They succeeded because they always acted with an abundance mindset. They sincerely believed there was plenty of opportunity to go around, so why not help someone else climb? In fact, they abandoned the metaphor of climbing the ladder completely and embraced the idea of climbing the jungle gym, with space for all. Every successful woman in these pages shares that defining trait: they not only fought hard to get where they are, but they also reached back to ease another's path.

I have seen proof that this matters in every step of my career. A lot of powerful women—and men—have paved the way for me to achieve my goals, and the gratitude I feel suffuses every aspect of my life. I wake up every morning and make a conscious choice to pull other people up.

We're so close to a world of equality, opportunity, and diversity for all. We can't screw it up now. It will take women at every stage of their entrepreneurial journey to keep us moving forward. Only when women at all levels come together can we survive and thrive. Through the stories in this book, those who have already walked the founder's path and those who follow will be inspired to become active members of a tribe—a movement that provides tools, a support network, and planning in the service of innovation.

The world becomes a better place when great ideas are brought to fruition. Women owe it to themselves and to the world to fight the odds against them. It is only then that we have an opportunity to change the world for the better.

The powerful and passionate women profiled in this book show the way.

—Kelley Steven-Waiss

Chapter 1

MYTHS OF SUCCESSFUL FOUNDERS

WHY TOMORROW'S FOUNDERS WON'T LOOK LIKE YESTERDAY'S

> *SWAY is female-founded, owned, and run because I like a competitive advantage.*
>
> **—DENISE BROUDER, FOUNDER, SWAY**

Denise Brouder is a deep thinker on the future of work, and she believes that future is female. "Just from an economic perspective," she explains. "There are more female college graduates currently in the US workforce than college-educated males, and more women are currently earning higher education degrees than men, two indicators that the workplace is fundamentally shifting toward women."

But for Brouder, it's not just about numbers.

She says,

In today's market, if you want to acquire a customer, you have to think radically differently. Consumers want to know that we get them. To do that, we have to be highly empathetic, not aggressive. We have to change our whole way of how we see people.

This essential skill, she believes, is "most present in females. So that is our competitive advantage."

She's not alone in thinking women are on the rise and adding value to the bottom line. Impact investor Nancy Pfund, founder and managing partner of DBL Partners, sees in her work that "healthy financial performance and positive social change are inherently connected." Part of that social change is the inclusion of female founders. She observes that "there are more women starting companies than there used to be, and there's more enthusiasm for these women." Her fund tracks the percentage of their portfolio of female CEOs and C-suites, and while the national average hovers around 10 percent, at the time of this writing, their fund was around 63 percent. Pfund has seen firsthand that seeking out and investing in women-founded firms like The RealReal, Ruby Ribbon, and Urban Sitter has been good business. Recent research from McKinsey & Company confirms that companies that have gender diversity on executive teams were 25 percent more likely to have above-average profitability.[2]

But while it's clear to many that women are changing the face of American business for the better, the message isn't getting through

---

2 Sundiatu Dixon-Fyle, Kevin Dolan, Dame Vivian Hunt, and Sara Prince, "Diversity wins: How inclusion matters," McKinsey & Company, May 19, 2020, https://www.mckinsey.com/featured-insights/diversity-and-inclusion/diversity-wins-how-inclusion-matters.

to everyone. Inherent bias persists. The clichés of how successful founders should look and act are still entrenched: the lone wolf, the MBA/finance guru, the get-rich-quick genius, the fearless risk-taker, and so on. These myths are stereotypes that keep deserving ideas from getting recognized. If we're going to move the needle on who's getting funded and who's not, we need to revise our thinking around who is seen as a potential founder and who isn't.

Sometimes, we're even our own worst enemies. It's important for female entrepreneurs themselves to not buy into the myths. If someone had told me when I was young that I would grow up to not only lead people but also change the world by building a technology platform that would revolutionize the way people work, I would have said they were crazy. The world continually told me that what I brought to the table wasn't relevant in the realms of business and entrepreneurship. For too long, I listened to them. For too long, others listened, too.

It's time to change our thinking. My story and the story of Hitch is an example of a new way forward.

MYTH:
Successful Founders Are Sharks

REALITY:
Successful Founders Are Dolphins

I didn't grow up with a lot of money, and neither of my parents graduated college in their youth. My parents divorced when I was only seven years old, and both worked in average-paying jobs, my father as a struggling sound producer and my mother as a bookkeeper. As I got older, instead of staying in after school care, I would shadow my grandfather, Bill Steven, or one of my three great uncles who ran our small family business in the San Fernando Valley, called Steven's Nursery and Hardware. On school holidays, I would help out at the store sorting nails, watering plants, or sweeping up—and always, observing how the family managed what felt like a big operation to me.

One day, an old lady brought a dead plant into the store and insisted on talking only to my grandfather. She then proceeded to complain that the plant had died despite all her best care. Without the slightest hesitation, my grandfather kindly offered to give her another plant. After she left, I said to my grandfather, "She's probably going to kill that plant, too. You're just going to have to give her another one." He said, "That's OK. She's been a very good customer for over forty years. It's the right thing to do."

Eight-year-old me was just incensed by that. I thought that she was taking advantage of my grandfather. I thought that he was losing money, and business was all about making money. I didn't understand it at all.

Now I understand that my grandfather had an abundance mindset. He came to the world with the attitude that there was enough for everyone. He was happy to give something away to a loyal customer not only because he hoped that she'd come back for a bigger pot or a watering can but also because he hoped that she'd learn to love and care for plants the way he did. He wanted to create a world where people could appreciate what flowers, trees, and landscaping would add to our community. I was living in a scarcity mindset, protective, with a negative attitude about the nature of people, thinking everything was transactional, and my behavior followed suit.

From years of watching my grandfather and other important mentors throughout my career, I learned to live in that abundance mindset where there's plenty of room for everybody to win. We're all in it together. There will always be bad actors in every corner, but my grandfather showed me that if you shift your thinking to abundance versus scarcity, amazing things happen. Suddenly, you have the ability to think bigger, past the potential loss of revenue to repeat, happy customers, and a world full of foliage. He showed me that when you become more gracious to other people, you create room to mentor and help them. One day, that lady would learn to keep a plant alive with a little help from my grandfather, and then the sky's the limit: a whole garden, perhaps! By showing her kindness and grace, he not only helped his business, but he also helped make the world a better place by sharing his passion freely.

> If you shift your thinking to abundance versus scarcity, amazing things happen.

This sort of thinking became a part of me, and without it, I never would have gotten my tech company, Hitch, off the ground. As you'll see in these pages, the abundance mindset helped me at every stage of my entrepreneurial journey. Every story in this book manifests that pattern.

One great example of ditching the shark mindset for abundance thinking is the story of Ashley Reid and her company, Wellist. While a student at Carnegie Mellon, Ashley lived through her mother's illness with cancer. At the time she thought, *there's this thing called the internet. It shouldn't be so hard for my sick mother to get a toddler to school and dinner on the table.* When Reid's best friend's father was diagnosed with cancer over a decade later, Reid was struck by how little had changed. She left her corporate job to found Wellist, a technology company with a mission to help hospitals, patients, and their families coordinate and access services at times of crisis. When COVID-19 hit in 2020, Wellist was suddenly confronted with a new reality. Reid says:

> We were losing cash because hospitals were in trouble. We were losing customers because my teams couldn't go to work. More importantly, people were dying at just horrifying rates. Chelsea was the hardest-hit neighborhood in Boston where we were based. People were sitting in their cars or standing in the cold for hours to get a PCR test. We felt strongly that there was an opportunity for us to help. Even though we were losing money, we hired people to go out to those long lines and help people find the information and services they needed. We also opened our platform for free to nurses to help them find childcare and other help with daily tasks. We didn't have money. It wasn't clear how this was going to go. But I felt very strongly that our moral imperative was to show up and do this, and so that's what I decided to do. I didn't have an off button on that.

Reid's investors and board got behind her, and in the end, Wellist won the MassTLC COVID Response of the Year Award, gaining them priceless PR. That, as well as the relationships and knowledge they accrued during the crisis, allowed them to come out of the pandemic stronger and more focused than before. This was the abundance mindset in action.

MYTH:
Founders Go It Alone

REALITY:
Founders Create Allies

Part of an abundance mindset is the belief that everyone can help someone else. In elementary school and junior high, I wasn't popular at all. I was the girl in glasses, the smart kid, super nerdy. And when you were smart, you were ostracized. I was that kid who leaned back in her chair and had it pulled out from under her. I remember it being very awkward during those years, even when I finally found a friend as equally geeky as me. Then, we were both ostracized together. It was pretty painful for me in those early days. I cried almost every day. I told myself I would never treat other people that way.

As I got older, into high school, I grew into myself and found my place in the world. I became a dancer, an athlete, and I lost the glasses. I did theater, writing, and art. By high school, being the smart, creative kid had its perks, and I had plenty of friends. Still, I remained the one who noticed the girl who always sat by herself at lunch. That empathy had stayed with me. I would go and sit with her or pull her into my group. *There's room for everyone.* I never forgot how it felt to be alone.

Throughout my career, the more success I had, the more I pulled other people up with me. Whether it was the start of my career when I worked in retail or later when I became the CEO of a tech company, most of the women who worked for me are still a part of my network, and that's helped them go on to much bigger roles. It came back to help me, too, in ways I never expected, even though that wasn't why I did it. When it came time to start my company, I had so many people of varied talents to call on for help, support, and advice.

It's a myth that most founders are lone wolves, eccentric and moody people who don't work well with others. Sure, I had some really bad experiences in my career with women who didn't support me or didn't help me. In truth, they did exactly the opposite. But what I learned from my journey is that successful founders build networks of mentors, mentees, partners, friends, and advisors. They have a true desire to help other people, to collaborate, and to include. For every Mark Zuckerberg as mythologized in *The Social Network*, there's a Sara Blakely, the founder of Spanx, who sees her business as a platform "to do what my greater mission and goal is, which is to help women in a big way."[3] The ability to build a team is the mark of a great founder, and it starts on day one.

MYTH:
Founders Are Born

REALITY:
Founders Are Made

After college, I graduated into a major recession. My dream was to be a journalist, but there were no jobs as a reporter, so I ended up taking a job at The Limited, Inc. in their management rotation program. I was dropped into a retail store as an assistant manager and had to figure out how to do merchandising, operations, customer service, staffing, and inventory. I was back on the shop floor. I wasn't proud of that.

---

3   Lindzi Scharf, "Spanx Founder Sara Blakely gives back to empower women, small businesses," Variety Magazine, October 10, 2016, https://variety.com/2016/biz/features/sarah-blakely-spanx-women-small-businesses-1201884257/.

I didn't aspire to work in retail, but I knew how to be successful in that environment because I grew up in it. I stayed in retail for a long time. I worked for Nike, Ann Taylor, Roots of Canada, Nordstrom, and Gap. And I eventually moved to Gap headquarters after I had been in the field for many, many years. I felt as if I had really paid my dues, but it still wasn't my "be-all and end-all."

Despite feeling that I was not where I wanted to be, having an abundance mindset made me an optimistic person, the kind of person who always looked for the silver lining. Even though managing a retail store wasn't my dream job, it taught me how a business ran and how to respect the people who worked for me. Often, my employees were ten or more years older than me. I had to figure out how to show up as a leader, managing and evaluating them while still giving them the respect they deserved. It wasn't hard because I truly believed they deserved respect. It wasn't a stretch for me. They were good people, and there was an important and valuable role for us all.

One aspect of my retail career that stayed with me was the belief that everyone was so much more than the job they were in at that point in time. I wasn't exactly where I wanted to be, and I knew many of my employees weren't either. I respected people for their potential. I held a strong belief that everyone should be able to pursue their passions and to reimagine themselves.

Everyone should be able to bring their whole selves to their work. I was motivated to learn, grow, and pursue my passions and interests, and I tried to spark that spirit in the people I worked with. My message was that every experience helps someone to move forward. As far as I was concerned, none of us were stuck, but rather we were all learning, opening new opportunities for ourselves and for one another. It was an early lesson on the "growth mindset," something I would later learn to appreciate from the work of Carol Dweck at Stanford.

This thinking was amplified when during this time, my mother left her job to enter the Los Angeles Police Department. This was unheard of—a female police officer starting out at forty-five years old. She had always dreamed of entering the force like her father before her, and she went for it fearlessly. She didn't exactly sail through the grueling academy, and despite her age and the physical challenges of the academy, she graduated at the top of her class and won the Tina Kerbrat Award for most inspirational cadet.

Three days after graduating from the police academy, she was killed in the line of duty while responding to a domestic violence dispute. The shock of the tragedy and the emotional chaos that followed were devastating. Yet, I eventually found some peace in knowing that she'd had the opportunity to pursue her lifelong dream. As I worked through the pain, her bravery would become one of the strongest and most meaningful takeaways from her loss. It defined the rest of my life's work. My mother's experience taught me that being able to reimagine yourself, pursue your passions, and be recognized as being able to contribute in a second act was a worthwhile and noble goal.

Losing her became the final catalyst that solidified my belief that people are not fixed beings; they have the ability to change and grow over time. This was a transformative perspective. I had found my passion: to find a way to bring the growth mindset to organizations and apply it. Eventually, this led to Hitch, my software start-up that facilitated employees' growth and mobility within organizations.

WHAT IS HITCH?

hitch™

Hitch is a SaaS solution that leverages skills intelligence to drive greater internal talent mobility and growth. It helps companies become more adaptive and innovative by connecting the right talent with the right tasks or roles based on employee skills, experiences, career goals, and location. Hitch matches the skills and passions of employees with organizational needs so that business opportunities—whether project-based or full-time—can be resourced from within.

This internal marketplace creates a culture of learning, growth, and engagement where people feel valued, and the organization achieves greater productivity and performance while retaining its most valuable talent assets. By connecting the right people's skills at the right time to the right place, organizations can rapidly respond to the demanding nature of today's economy. People's skills become visible and mobile while supporting a personalized career development journey based on their own aspirations.

We created Hitch to unleash the talent inside, for both an organization and its people.

Founding a company is hard—harder than anything else you'll ever do in business. Life is hard—it beats us back in unexpected and seemingly devastating ways. It's a myth that entrepreneurs are born. They're made. They're an embodiment of every challenge they've faced. Turning even the most overwhelming setbacks into inspiration to move forward is one of the most important marks of an entrepreneur. And yet, it goes against the myth of the golden child, always the smartest person in the room, destined for greatness from day one. Let's eliminate that idea and instead see the worth in people's struggles and lessons learned along a rockier path.

MYTH:
Founders Must Be Financial Pros

REALITY:
Founders Are Creatives

Founders need to have vision and connect the dots. To do that, they need to be creative thinkers. I carried around notepads wherever I went, and when I got an idea, I would draw it out and create mind maps and all kinds of diagrams. Sometimes my notes would be about branding or taglines. Other times, I'd create lists of all the ways to create use cases for the technology I envisioned.

While I worked for Gap, I also got a master's degree in organization development, which was training in change management and systemic thinking. It demanded constant creativity. When Gap wouldn't let me move into an organizational development (OD) role, I got a job with the firm Watson Wyatt Worldwide (now called Willis Towers Watson), a global human resource consulting firm. I joined the Organization Effectiveness practice and worked on corporate culture transformation projects. That led to a career in HR, which ultimately led me to tech where I started working with iconic companies like Cisco Systems.

My new roles put the bug in my ear about high tech, which was fascinating, complex, and fast-moving. Eventually, after consulting for years, I was asked to take a chief human resources officer (CHRO) role, a title I held for the next thirteen years. I became the instantiation of everything I was building. My gift was my ability to be a disruptor against the status quo, creative and unconstrained in connecting all my experiences into big-picture ideas. I became a thought leader, a regular keynote speaker on the future-of-work circuit. We knew big changes were coming, and we had to think creatively to imagine models that didn't yet exist.

Creativity enabled me at every step of this journey. I would never have been able to stand up in front of a room and deliver a keynote without my theater training. If I wasn't a good writer, I wouldn't have been a good change agent or communicator. Yet, I didn't have a background that necessarily impressed venture capitalists. At first, no one was jumping up to open their wallets. Venture is attracted to people with financial discipline, business acumen, and credentials. Often, financial people are not the creatives. They can crunch numbers, but they're not usually the ones who come up with the next big idea, at least most of the time. They're not waking up in the middle of the night jotting their ideas in a notebook, whiteboarding and drawing mind maps, and imagining what might be.

I had run businesses since I was out of college, and running businesses meant understanding how to make money. But none of that counted when trying to get funding. My real secret weapons were the skills I had underneath the surface. I was really good at marketing, and yet investors often can't evaluate those skills in the pitching process.

However, I knew how to build a brand, which turns out to be priceless. Ultimately, the value of my company was largely based on the brand that we had built. People thought we were a much bigger company because of how analysts were talking about Hitch and how the brand showed up. That was leaning into my creative edge.

When I pitched Hitch, I was turned down by at least forty-plus venture firms. The fiftieth-something saw my potential, saw outside the usual box, and bet on me. I don't want to give away the ending, but he wasn't sorry. That was the value of seeing outside the myths.

MYTH:
Founders Are Inherent Risk-Takers

REALITY:
Founders Manage Risk

Before I got that first check, however, I had walked another nontraditional path.

After I had finally gotten my big idea for Hitch, my plan was to cut the corporate cord and go out on my own to make it real. I was planning to be an entrepreneur. Then a friend asked me to interview with a CEO who was looking for a CHRO. I turned him down. I said, "I'm going to pitch investors on an idea that I have. I'm really not looking for the next CHRO role."

He pushed anyway, so I met the CEO of HERE Technologies, Edzard Overbeek, for lunch in Los Altos. We hit it off right away. I told him about my idea for a start-up (see the section on allies and having an abundance mindset), and he loved it. He was an accredited investor who had recently invested in technology adjacent to what I had in mind. We went back and forth, and he eventually said, "If you come in as the CHRO of HERE, we will internally support you with resources at the experiment stage, and we'll see if it works. This can be your lab."

At this point, I was in my late forties. I had four kids with college education still in the future. I was the breadwinner of my family. I was planning to build Hitch "in my garage" à la Steve Jobs and make no money for a while. If I went into HERE as an intrapreneur, I wouldn't have to put my family's welfare at risk. I talked to my husband, and we decided being an intrapreneur was the right thing for us at the time.

WHAT IS AN INTRAPRENEUR?

An intrapreneur is someone who builds their idea inside another company. This allows them to use the existing structures and resources to iterate and de-risk their concept with support. I started my journey as an intrapreneur and ended it as an entrepreneur after I spun Hitch out.

This was early in 2016. Later, after I got ownership of Hitch back, got venture funding, and spun it out on my own, I realized how lucky I was to have gone forward the way I did. In 2015, women did not get funding on ideas—ever. After I had spent five years making an executive salary while also building the product, revenue, and customers, I still could barely get funding even though I had been essentially de-risked inside a large enterprise. If I had gone out on my own in 2016, I'd have been too early, not just for the market but also for the myths, which were still firmly in place. I wasn't a shark. I wasn't a lone wolf. I wasn't "born to lead." I wasn't an MBA. I wasn't a wild risk-taker.

But I *was* a founder. And maybe you are, too. Don't let anyone tell you you're not.

The Marks of a Founder

Successful founders are collaborators and creative and passion- and mission-led leaders with an abundance mindset who support one another and take calculated, smart risks when the conditions are right. All these modes of operating in the business world are considered primarily "female" traits. In other words, tomorrow's founders are likely to be women.

The first step to becoming a founder is knowing that you're OK the way you are—there's success in embracing your "female" super-powers. Women don't have to force themselves into the old paradigms.

The next step is to hold onto those values as you bring your big idea out into the world.

LESSONS FROM FEMALE FOUNDERS:
Myth Busting

I was born in Rwanda, then grew up in Tanzania and Zambia. My father couldn't read or write. Potential employers would see that, then make assumptions about whether or not he was able to do a job. So he thought, "I can't fit in the traditional mold, so I will create my own destiny." Before the genocide, he was one of the most successful entrepreneurs I ever knew. Now, I see the same attitudes in traditional VCs toward me. They see me, a Black woman, and think, 'Oh, traditionally we haven't seen models of that, so therefore we won't be able to invest.' We need to change that. We need to be telling VCs to open the door a little wider. Check your assumptions. Let more kinds of people in.

—ANONYMOUS FOUNDER

We are all the same. We have the same levels of fear. Of ambition. There is so much equality between humans. But then we create labels. We go to our sides of the room, and then we can't even talk. I think it's all complete and utter bullshit.

—DENISE BROUDER, FOUNDER, SWAY

Everyone knows that we all carry implicit biases, and so some of those biases are going to be directed toward newcomers to a field when you're used to doing things the same old, same old. But I do think that there's a lot more awareness of the venture community now that implicit bias does exist. So, there's more effort being made to correct that and to hold firm that a big part of being a good founder is simply being someone who recognizes that they have to outsmart the status quo.

—NANCY PFUND, FOUNDER AND MANAGING PARTNER, DBL PARTNERS

Chapter 2

TAKING FLIGHT

THE IMPETUS, THE WHITEBOARD, AND
HOW TO ENSURE YOUR IDEA WILL FLY

> *Be passionate about the problem and flexible*
> *with the solution. It's very unlikely that the*
> *first idea that comes to your mind is going to*
> *be the one that takes you all the way.*
>
> **—MACKENZIE BRANIGAN, CEO AND CO-FOUNDER, GATHERMADE**

One sunny afternoon, in the spring of 2014, I was sitting outside at my favorite Mediterranean restaurant in San Jose, California and mulling over one of the biggest problems in HR. I was CHRO of a Silicon Valley tech company, and we were losing good people. It wasn't just us. The problem was everywhere. We knew that employees were constantly learning, growing, and developing, but their jobs stayed the same. Because of this, employees ended up bringing 60 percent of themselves to work, meaning their other 40 percent was not engaged. For a company, that's a lot of capacity left on the table. For employees, that's a reason to be unhappy, vote with their feet, and move on. Lose-lose.

I ate my lunch and thought through the problem:

How can our company visualize all the great talent that we have?

If people were more than the job they were currently doing, how could we understand their skills, capabilities, and aspirations?

How could we create more agility in the organization while giving people better access to opportunities (such as internal gigs) where they could contribute?

I knew the answer was not just about technology because getting access to skills information would likely be a huge change. For employees to share their data, there needed to be some exchange of value. I also knew that beyond the change in mindset or operating models, the technology didn't exist.

How could we create the simple, easy-to-use, flawless solution we needed?

What would it look like?

How would it work?

I had so many ideas, but I was plagued by not being able to articulate what it was that I could envision. And, as always, I had to get back to my day job. As I finished my lunch, I glanced up into the blue, cloudless California sky. Birds were flying in a V formation. Suddenly, the wind shifted, and they effortlessly reconfigured into two smaller V's going in a completely different direction. I thought, *That's it!*

I knew.

I'm a visual person. It's how my mind works. All at once, those birds opened my eyes to the solution. This was the analogy that connected all the dots for me. I knew exactly what I needed to create. I knew now what an internal talent marketplace would look like: a tech platform where people could take on projects within the company across divisions and even continents, shifting and changing roles *like birds, flying in formation.*

I hurried back to the office and somehow got through the rest of the afternoon, my idea scratching at the edges of my consciousness. As soon as the workday was over, I locked myself in the CEO's conference room, faced a blank whiteboard, and began to draw out the concept of a new operating model for talent leveraging a platform that matched peoples' skills to project based work in a marketplace. I also drew that echelon—OK, maybe in those hours after lunch, I'd stolen a moment or two to learn that birds flying in formation had a name. *Echelon.*

Nice name for a tech start-up, I thought.

I texted one of my CHRO mentors and asked her to come over, *now.* We were part of a CHRO group called CHREATE that was tasked with defining the impact of the future of work on the future of our profession. She had also been a CHRO for decades and was really a big thinker. She had been on the future-of-work circuit with me for years. I needed validation that I wasn't nuts.

My idea could work, right? It was big, wasn't it?

She met me in the conference room, and we shut the door behind us. I explained the birds and how they modeled the organization I wanted to create. She got it right away and was as excited as I was. We talked and drew, erased, and revised. We knew we were creating something unique that solved a big problem. We went back and forth from birds to organizational systems until we had the start of what seemed like an obvious and elegant solution.

At one point, I half-jokingly said,

I know it sounds crazy, but Tom Siebel, co-founder of Siebel Systems, once told us that when he and Pat House had started their company, he saved the flip charts of their first drawings. Tom had said, "If you ever have an idea, take a picture of it. You never know what's going to happen with that idea. It might actually turn into a company."

I snapped that picture with my iPhone, savoring the moment. After years of searching for the big idea, I had it, and now, it was time to make it real. I wasn't naïve. I knew it would be a struggle, but I was ready. For the past two decades, I had climbed the ranks of corporate America. It was a tough haul. What makes you successful as an executive is a combination of intelligence, creativity, passion, and empathy. It would take all these skills to transform that nugget of an idea in 2014 into a working system for the future of work.

This was my chance to use all my skills to change not just my company but also the world. I was at the top of my game. Like those birds, I was ready to fly.

How hard could it be?

It's Harder than You Think—but You've Got This

If I had known how hard it was going to be to take Hitch from idea to reality, I may not have done it. The thrill of the big idea was exhilarating, but what came next—not so much.

I urge people with big ideas to pause, savor, and celebrate this first step on the entrepreneurial journey. Then, it's time to get to work honing your initial thinking. You're not looking for perfection. Instead, you need to get moving on seeking iterative feedback from multiple sources. If you wait for perfection, you're not an entrepreneur. Entrepreneurship is about rapid iteration and experimentation. Perfection will be the death of innovation and speed. You need to look at the problem from different angles and make sure you understand why this

> **If you wait for perfection, you're not an entrepreneur.**

problem needs to be solved. For example, I wanted to solve for making organizations more agile and allowing more democratization. Hitch became the "how" on making that a reality, and it went through many iterations before it reached its final form. Only through this iterative process can you eventually hit on a solid foundation for moving forward.

There are plenty of resources that outline the basics of vetting ideas: looking for the problem, not the solution; looking for weakness in the competition; and so on. Here, however, my goal is to focus on the unique pitfalls that women face more often than men at the concept and whiteboarding phases. Avoiding these traps is the first step to leveling the playing field.

Women Need to Think Bigger

In Pitchbook's 2022 comprehensive report, "All In: Female Founders in the US VC Ecosystem," the data is clear: access to VC (venture capital) funding is historically more difficult for female founders.[4] In addition, according to a decade-long study by Crunchbase on median and average seed and Series A rounds, when women do find funding, female founders tend to raise less than their male counterparts.[5] Consider this a challenge, not an obstacle. You must be clear-eyed and realistic about what is ahead of you, but don't let that limit you. The bar is higher for women, so you need a big idea that solves a big problem if you're going to clear it.

> The most important lesson at the ideation stage of your start-up is to give yourself the freedom to THINK BIG.

The most important lesson at the ideation stage of your start-up is to give yourself the freedom to THINK BIG.

Don't give yourself any constraints. Don't talk yourself out of why something's not going to work. Draw it out in free form. Put it in a PowerPoint. Draw it on a whiteboard. (Then take a picture of it for posterity.) Put it on a napkin, a flip chart, or a voice memo. Invite

---

4   Pitchbook, "All in: Female founders in the US VC ecosystem," November 2, 2022, PDF, 3, https://pitchbook.com/news/reports/2022-all-in-female-founders-in-the-us-vc-ecosystem.

5   Crunchbase, "Funding the female founders," March, 2020, PDF, 5, https://www.google.com/search?q=crunchbase+%22funding+to+female+founders%22+report&oq=crunchbase+%22funding+to+female+founders%22+report&aqs=chrome..69i57j69i64.11196j0j4&sourceid=chrome&ie=UTF-8.

someone to come over who is also a big thinker and supportive of you to get their opinion. Combine all the smaller ideas that you have into one, and let it free flow. Your first idea may not be the final idea, nor should it be. You should spend the time to make it grow as big as possible before you take the next steps.

Ask yourself:

- *What is the problem my big idea can solve? Is the problem big enough?*

- *How can this be applicable in more markets?*

- *How can I flip this from a product to a service?*

- *How is this going to displace the incumbent in this field?*

The idea stage is the time to dream. Big.

Women Need to Find Their Flock

In her groundbreaking 2003 book, *She Wins, You Win*, Gail Evans points out that women network differently than men:

> We get information ... all the time from our (social) networks, except at work, where we back down because here we think we're supposed to make it entirely on our own. Women are struggling with this concept because we think that using a friend to achieve some positive result in business is nasty, immoral, and manipulative. We don't understand that having a close friend to help you make a business contact is a routine favor that men do for each other all the time.[6]

---

6   Gail Evans, *She Wins, You Win* (New York: Gotham Books, 2003), 37.

Amazingly, in the twenty years since Evans wrote these words, not much has changed. I still see women hobbled by trying to go it alone. The idea stage is the time to assemble your flock. Don't wait. You need people who will poke holes in the idea as well as those who will help you get over those objections. Every objection could send you down another path of discovery or analysis. I didn't have all the answers for how to build my idea into Hitch, but I did know how to ask really good questions of people in my network who had more experience in their area of expertise. As Evans says, men tend to do this naturally. Women need to catch up.

When I had my big idea for Hitch, I had an established network. If you don't have one, form one. I called it my "personal board of directors." Attend networking events and conferences. If you do have a network, this is the chance to analyze, build, and maintain it. You need people who have different backgrounds and disciplines. For Hitch, I talked to technologists, businesspeople, branding experts, finance folks, venture capitalists, and just plain old good, smart friends over glasses of wine. I asked broad questions like, *What do you think of this? Is this crazy?* And I asked specific questions to those with expertise. For example, I would sit down with my marketing friends and say, "I had an idea of how I would position the company, but what do you think? You're the expert in this."

CEO and Founder Ashley Reid advises,

When I coach other female entrepreneurs, I say, "Your first job is to go talk to thirty people in thirty days. None of them can be an investor. Your goal is to ask as many questions as you can, and then go back and try and put it together, because at the end of that time you will have so much more information."

Set yourself networking goals and stick to them:

- Make a list of your network and look for the gaps. Who are you missing? Branding? Tech? Go out and find that person now, and then buy them lunch.

- Remember that your contacts have contacts. Don't be afraid to ask. Your mantra should always be, *The worst they can say is no.*

- Founder Sheila Talton advises, "Don't just look to your peers. When you meet people who are in high places, think about how you can be of service to them."

Women Need to Build a Personal Platform

Men are often instantly seen as founders because they fit the mold. Women need to build their personal brand from day one. Talking to a lot of people about your idea is one way to do this. Of course, you're probably thinking, *shouldn't I keep it a secret? What if someone steals my idea?* When you embrace the abundance mindset—that there's enough for everyone and people are generally good and helpful— you'll avoid seeing everyone as your competitor and feel better about getting yourself out there and getting loud.

While I built Hitch, I remained an evangelist about the value of an internal talent marketplace. I didn't do my work under the shroud of secrecy. I was constantly on stage talking about my ideas and what we were doing to change HERE Technologies ("HERE"). I spoke about the solutions that we had built in front of thousands of business and HR leaders. I was building my credibility in the future-of-work conversation as an expert. People listened to me. I even wrote my first book, *The Inside Gig*, about this new way of working. I was part of the "movement."

Sure, if somebody on the outside was as fired up about my idea as I was, they could have stolen my idea and built a venture-backed company before I did. In fact, while I was still an intrapreneur, building Hitch as part of HERE, one of my main competitors, GLOAT, emerged. Around the same time, Rally Team out of San Francisco also got acquired by WorkDay. They may have heard of me or may not have, but it didn't matter. By then, I had been on the front lines for years, making contacts and speaking from a place of sharing, abundance, and passion. I had been the face of internal talent marketplaces for years before I spun out Hitch. When I came out venture-backed in 2020, I was a dark horse. By that time, I hadn't just defined my company, but I had also established myself as a practitioner and thought leader. As you'll see in later chapters, my brand and profile became a key element in the success of transitioning from an intrapreneur to an entrepreneur. Even though I wasn't the first to market, I was instantly recognized and respected as a player in the game. That doesn't happen by quietly executing and hoping the market notices.

FOUR WAYS TO BUILD A PLATFORM AROUND YOUR BRAND:

WRITE A BOOK

My book, *The Inside Gig*, started out as a lead magnet and ended up as a calling card I could give to potential investors. Nothing says "thought leader" better than a book.

SPEAK AT CONFERENCES

I was a huge evangelist and thought leader for my product and the problem it could solve, speaking wherever I could about my vision for an internal talent marketplace and the strategy for organizations to move to a skills-based operating model.

CREATE YOUR OWN MOVEMENT

If it doesn't exist, build it. Adriana Gascoigne founded her nonprofit, Girls in Tech, to share experiences with other women in Silicon Valley, and ended up creating the largest organization for female entrepreneurs in the world.

RAISE YOUR VOICE

ALearn founder Kathryn Hanson advises:

> Stand up and participate in meetings and management as if you are meant to be there (you are). Don't let it get to you if you are questioned and just participate as an equal with men and people higher up. Be active. Do your homework well before you walk into the room for meetings.

Women Need to Create Value

While I was creating a platform for the company, I was also creating a market for Hitch. I'll never know what would have happened if I had kept my idea under "stealth mode" and done less external evangelism, but in hindsight, I believe speaking up was the right thing to do. Of course, while I was creating a market, I was also creating more competition. The founders of GLOAT were all men, and so they got a lot of backing from a lighthouse customer evangelizing for them and got early access to funding. As a female-founded company at such an early stage, that would have been a very tall order for Hitch.

I choose to see the situation as a glass half full. The laws of economics tell us that once there's competition, there's a market. I knew we had created a true market when Gartner analysts covered it as an emerging category called ITM or Internal Talent Marketplace. That was the solution I first whiteboarded in 2014 when the category didn't exist. I know I played a crucial role in evolving that category, and in the end, all the emerging competition was only to my benefit.

HOW TO BUILD VALUE:

VALUE COMES FROM HOW YOU DEFINE, DESCRIBE, AND EVANGELIZE AROUND YOUR IDEA

It takes time and trial and error to get your message just right. The only way to do that is to get out there and test it.

VALUE MUST BE DEMONSTRATED

I was getting on stage, showing the problem statement, how I broke down the problem, the solution that I had for the problem, and how it worked. I had all the proof points.

VALUE IS CONFIRMED BY HAVING CUSTOMERS

Identify others who have the problem statement and who need to solve the problem but don't have the technology to do it. Then sell it.

VALUE COMES FROM STIMULATING DEMAND

Sometimes, very novel things work. No one was screaming for an iPhone when Steve Jobs came out with the first. The key is that it doesn't have to be something that the market is asking for, but it has to be solving a problem, even if everyone doesn't yet know they had a problem. I was stimulating demand by talking about the need to create a new workplace operating model. I was building the demand and then answering it with my technology. Talton was stimulating demand for diverse players in healthcare and then backing it up by helping others coming up behind her.

Women Need to Lean into Their Passion

If you don't care about the problem you're solving, it's just not going to work. You're not going to have the patience to figure it out.

—JODY MADALA, CEO AND FOUNDER

You can work for money, but if you're pursuing your idea as a means to getting rich, you'll never survive the roller-coaster highs and lows of being a female entrepreneur. It's like any relationship. In your heart, you must be so passionate that you'll walk through walls to get it done. If it's just about the money or taking shortcuts, you'll never push through, especially if you're a woman because there are simply more obstacles in your path.

When I first started in tech, everyone would talk about their prior "exits" or their current "path to IPO." There was suddenly the strong possibility that you could be a few years out of college and have a shortcut to wealth. People saw Silicon Valley as a gold mine. Come in with a great idea, and it doesn't matter how much experience you have—you can make it big. This motivation drove innovation, but it also created the delusion that tech entrepreneurship was the fast and easy way to infinite riches. While many people did find a path to wealth in the early days, winning doesn't usually happen that easily.

For women, it's even more rare because often that kind of get-rich-quick win is based on luck—that is, on being in the right place at the right time while also ideally having a huge (mostly male) network with access to capital.

While you may not have that going for you, I believe that women are lucky in other ways. For one, they tend to embrace entrepreneurial ideas that grow from their passions and mission, not the pursuit of money. Women need to lean into this, not away from it.

For example, Adriana Gascoigne, CEO and founder of Girls in Tech, explains that

> the tech industry was exciting, fast-paced, and innovative ... But it was also rampant with sexual harassment and hostile toward women. If I was going to march on, I owed it to myself to build a support system. ... A bunch of assholes couldn't deter the sheer joy I experienced from building something. [7]

That passion for tech eventually led Gascoigne to found her international nonprofit in 2007, which now has over a hundred thousand members across six continents.

Women are often hesitant to frame their ideas around passion and purpose because they're told that entrepreneurship is all about money. My grandfather always told me, "Do what you love, and success will follow you." We need to embrace that narrative. It's OK to be passionate about outcomes other than profit. And when we are, profits often follow.

---

7   Adriana Gascoigne, *Tech Boss Lady* (Hachette Book Group, 2019: New York), xii-xvii.

TAKE TIME FOR A PASSION CHECK:

1. ARE YOU OBSESSED WITH SOLVING THE PROBLEM YOUR IDEA WILL ADDRESS?

I was so passionate about how Hitch could solve the win-win for employees and their organizations that even though I worked full-time at my day job and had four children, whenever I had a spare moment, Hitch was all I wanted to do. I really loved it, and I knew that when I loved something, I was a force to be reckoned with.

2. WHEN YOU WORK ON THE PROBLEM STATEMENT AND YOUR IDEA FOR THE SOLUTION, DO YOU ENTER A STATE OF FLOW?

When you really love something, you're so excited about it, you'll lose yourself in it. The time just goes by because you're loving what you're doing. It's the huge upside of your passion and obsession.

3. ARE YOU BUILDING MORE THAN A BUSINESS?

Entrepreneurship is hard. CEO and Founder Ashley Reid said, "I'd wake up every day and think about my mom and Susan's mom, and what it was like for her when she was struggling." That passion got her through.

Women Must Be the Champions of Their Ideas

I was a perfectionist, a notorious self-deprecator. I was always saying to myself, *What business do you have thinking YOU can build a technology company? Are you an engineer?* Women often experience this kind of imposter syndrome because the world is always telling us that we're not good enough. I'd say to myself, *You're crazy, Kelley, just because you're an outstanding communicator and you're so good at building a brand doesn't mean you can build a technology company.*

Based on observing the male founders around me, this doesn't seem to be as much of a problem for them. Neither Steve Jobs nor Mark Zuckerberg bothered to get college degrees or corporate experience before they launched. Yet they pushed through obstacle after obstacle, ignoring the people who told them their ideas wouldn't work. They seemed to have no doubts. They believed in themselves and their ideas completely.

Part of the reason for this is that they're not questioned in the way women are. One female founder compares her experience raising funds for her start-up with the experience of her partner, a white male. She says,

> He has this relaxed approach to being, this sureness. For him, an art school dropout, no one ever touches the question of what school he went to. For me, I can't count the number of times people ask me my qualifications when I walk into a room. There's such a difference in the way that men act with each other.

Her observations are backed up by research. Researchers at Tech-Crunch Disrupt New York City documented that

> investors tend to ask male entrepreneurs promotion-focused questions and female entrepreneurs prevention-focused questions … This distinction in the regulatory focus of investor questions and entrepreneur responses results in divergent funding outcomes for entrepreneurs whereby those asked promotion-focused questions raise significantly

higher amounts of funding than those asked prevention-focused questions.

They found that "every additional prevention-focused question significantly hinders the entrepreneur's ability to raise capital, fully mediating gender's effect on funding." To combat this, founders "can significantly increase funding for their start-ups when responding to prevention-focused questions with promotion-focused answers."[8]

In these situations, Allison Baum Gates, General Partner at SemperVirens Venture Capital, advises,

> Be prepared for that and understand how to direct the narrative so that you don't end up being led down a rabbit hole. I think one of the best things you can do as a founder pitching a VC is be prepared to control the conversation and to walk in with confidence and know exactly what you want to say and the messages you want to get across. Be in control.

Recognize that staying positive in the face of others' doubt isn't easy. Even Whitney Wolfe Herd, the founder of the lifestyle brand Bumble, told *Time Magazine* that she felt a "degree of imposter syndrome" on the day she became the youngest-ever female founder at thirty-one to take a company public with an initial $8.7B valuation. Despite her success, she said, "On a day like today, when everyone's celebrating, I'm still kind of looking over my shoulder, like, we have to do more."[9]

---

8   Dana Kanze, Laura Huang, Mark A. Conley, and E. Tory Higgins, "We Ask Men to Win and Women Not to Lose: Closing the Gender Gap in Startup Funding," *Academy of Management Journal* 61, no. 2 (April 20, 2018): 586–614. https://doi.org/10.5465/amj.2016.1215.

9   Charlotte Alter, "How Whitney Wolfe Herd Turned a Vision of a Better Internet into a Billion-Dollar Brand," Time Magazine, March 19, 2021, https://time.com/5947727/whitney-wolfe-herd-bumble/.

When Your Idea Is Ready for the World, Don't Hold Back

Once you're sure your idea is big enough, your platform and network are in place, your market is there, your passion is aligned with your idea, and you've overcome self-doubt, don't wait for your skillset. Trust yourself to rise to the occasion. I did this by always taking roles that scared me to death. After you've done that twenty times, you'll start to tell yourself a different story. You'll recognize that you've been in a place before where you've never done something—and then you do it. Founder Adriana Gascoigne of Girls in Tech says,

The world is full of competent people who honestly intend to do things tomorrow; however, tomorrow seldom comes for them. Many individuals with less talent are more successful because they understand the importance of urgency. In other words, get started now. [10]

LESSONS FROM FEMALE FOUNDERS
The Big Idea

We probably had a hundred different versions of our pitch deck. The weekend before demo day, I met with one of the leaders of the accelerator, and she said, "Don't freak out, but I think we need to change the entire deck and present it from the supply side not the customer side." We'd been working on this for a month, but that weekend, we changed the entire deck,

---

10   Adriana Gascoigne, *Tech Boss Lady*, 8.

and it was much stronger. The progression from where we started to where we finished was what made the difference.

—MACKENZIE BRANIGAN, CEO AND CO-FOUNDER, GATHERMADE

Companies who are coming of age now are going to be better served than a lot of companies when VC money was free and flowing because you're forced to think more carefully about what you're building. You have to ask, Am I building a sustainable long-term business versus just trying to catch a trend in the market and cash out? It's very important to be honest with yourself about why you're in the space.

—JODY MADALA, CEO AND FOUNDER, CULTURORA

The people we call visionaries are the ones who actually both see the vision and see the execution. When you think of who a visionary is, we only know of them because there was an execution. Everybody else is just dreaming and talking about their ideas at cocktail parties.

—DEIDRE PAKNAD, CEO AND CO-FOUNDER, WORKBOARD

Chapter 3

MOMENTS OF TRUTH

> *Having co-founders is like being married. I really liked them as people. They were smart and kind, but we just had different risk profiles and different hopes and visions of the future.*
>
> **—SALLY THORNTON, CEO AND FOUNDER, FORSHAY**

Sally Thornton was eight months pregnant with her first child when her older brother died in a plane crash. The experience changed her outlook on life. She had been working nonstop at a Silicon Valley tech company, but now she wanted to spend more time with her family. She said, "I was obsessed with work. I really, really liked it. I thought of it as an interesting game. How do I make money? How do I help people? It was a key game in life." But now, she felt as if "the rules were all wrong."

She wished that there was a way that an experienced, senior executive like herself could find flexible, project-based work that utilized her skills and training while still giving her access to a more balanced life. She had enough contacts and experience that she could become an independent consultant.

She explained,

> That would have been much easier, frankly. But I wanted to figure out how to do it for other people. That was a bigger motivation. I wanted my girlfriends in my mother's club to have access to the same life where work didn't consume life. I didn't want to be playing this work/life game alone.

She decided to build a company to make it happen. It was a big idea, and the company she co-founded based on it eventually became her first start-up, Flexperience. It got off to a great start, but soon she began experiencing differences with her two partners. While no one was right or wrong, their vision wasn't aligned.

"It was awful. My co-founders did not love the start-up life, and I get it. It's not for everyone, and you don't know until you try," Thornton remembered.

The co-founders decided to wind the company down at the same time her dad was diagnosed with cancer and her husband had been laid off. She was devastated. Thornton had a great idea; did the grueling, hard work to make it a reality; and then had to shut it down because of an early misstep: misaligned partners. Her co-founders decided to enforce a noncompete despite the company being closed, and Thornton took that time off to check in with her customers and consultants on whether her business was really solving a problem. Thornton was faced with her moment of truth: *would she do it again?* This time she named her company like other one-word professional services companies (e.g., McKinsey, Bain, and Deloitte), but it was named after her brother, (Will) Forshay, who was her inspiration. And this time, she did it on her own.

Thornton's experience isn't unusual. A lot can go wrong in the early stages of getting your start-up off the ground. Some problems can be overcome, while others, such as having the wrong partners, often cannot. Entrepreneurs are often so excited to get moving; they can make rash decisions—or no decisions at all because they haven't even considered that they might have options available to them. Then, when things get tough and their moment of truth comes, their problems feel too big to overcome.

To get past early setbacks, you need to give yourself every advantage possible so that your ideas aren't prematurely thwarted. The higher bar for female founders means that it's even more important for women to get everything right in this initial stage of development. The good news is that when women do set things up with intention, they find that they possess superpowers that actually give them an advantage. If you approach each early decision from your superpower, when your moment of truth arrives—as it surely will for all of us—you'll be prepared to move forward with confidence.

POSSIBLE SETBACK
Choosing the Wrong Environment

SUPERPOWER
Collaboration and Abundance Mindset

Finding the right environment for your idea is key, yet many early founders don't consider intrapreneurship—developing your idea inside an existing company. In chapter 4, we'll explore intrapreneurship in detail, but for now, it's important to note that the opportunity exists. I chose intrapreneurship when Edzard Overbeek, the CEO of HERE, agreed that if I was to join HERE as a CHRO, I could use the opportunity as a lab to get Hitch off the ground. That turned out to be the smartest decision I could have made. And yet, at the time, many of my advisors told me they thought I was making a huge mistake. *You'll lose ownership of your IP.* For me, as for many female founders, the choice was deeply personal. If I had stood firm on the old myths of founders (lone wolf, wild risk-taker) and ignored my superpowers (abundance mindset, collaboration), I would never have made the intrapreneurial choice, and I don't believe Hitch would exist today.

But intrapreneurship isn't always the right path. If you do decide to go out on your own, be sure you're not doing so from a position of scarcity, competitiveness, and fear of losing but from a place of an abundance mindset and power.

POSSIBLE SETBACK
Leading from Fear

SUPERPOWER
Leading from Purpose and Values

Successful female founders lead with purpose and values, a superpower that women can lean into for a competitive advantage. Yet, often in the whirlwind of early-stage excitement, there doesn't seem to be time to do something as "soft" as defining culture.

I urge founders to do it anyway. When I took the job as CHRO at HERE, the first thing I did was go on a ninety-day global listening and learning tour of the company—a fairly typical task for a new CHRO. Almost immediately, I realized that we needed to do a culture audit. I hired Bain & Company to help me do a deep dive. In June 2016, in Amsterdam, I delivered a keynote speech at the Senior Leadership Summit to 350 senior leaders of HERE about the good and bad in the company's culture. Although there was a lot of good, people wanted to feel more seen and heard. To fix this, I presented my strategy to involve employees in defining a new set of corporate values for HERE going forward. I also outlined how a new internal talent platform would be part of this process. At the end of the forty-five-minute keynote, I said, "If you are with me on defining this new culture, stand up."

I held my breath—and was gratified and relieved to get a standing ovation.

When you're just getting started, of course, you can't hire a world-class consulting firm to help you, and no one is going to stand up to clap and cheer when you plant your flag on your lonely hill. Still, you must take the time to think culture through, write it down, and then use it as a guiding light for every decision you make. Founder and CEO Ashley Reid counsels new entrepreneurs that they "need to be very clear about how they are going to show up when things get hard and what is going to lead their judgment, decision making, and leadership."

I agree completely because I saw it work with Hitch. Acting like a big company at the start gives you the best chance of eventually becoming one in the end.

Hitch's core values were adopted from HERE because we believed in those core values and wanted to give respect to the company that brought us to life and promoted a culture of innovation. We chose to keep those same values we had at HERE alive in our company as we pursued a new path as an independent company.

HITCH'S VISION, MISSION, AND VALUES

OUR VISION (WHY)

We strive to create boundless opportunities and value for people, teams, and leaders globally.

OUR MISSION (HOW)

To make work more meaningful and purpose-driven for people and organizations.

OUR VALUES (WHAT)

BE BOLD: Be an innovator and a creative problem solver

BE TRUE: Act with honesty and integrity—be transparent

LEARN FAST: Re-imagine yourself—with a growth mindset

GIVE BACK: Lead with empathy—be generous with time and resources

WIN TOGETHER: Be collaborative, inclusive, and solution oriented

DRIVE CUSTOMER VALUE: Be customer-centric, accessible, and responsive

POSSIBLE SETBACK:
Picking the Wrong Team

SUPERPOWER:
Valuing Teamwork

Part of the magic of clearly defining your purpose and values early and then leading with them is that when you do, like-minded people find you. My first team members, two engineers from HERE's IT organization, approached me during a coffee break after my speech in Amsterdam. They introduced themselves as Babu Chackrapani and Mauri Niininen.

Mauri said, "Your speech was inspiring. Do you want help building the software you'll need to capture people's skills and to define the culture?"

I said, "Absolutely. Yes. I would love that."

Later that week, I was sitting in the airport waiting for my plane home when I got an email from Mauri. His hobby was writing novels, and he had written a story describing what the future would look like if we were able to implement a talent platform just like the one I had described at my talk. I was amazed. This was a man who shared my vision. I responded immediately, writing, "I need to get you involved in this project." He wrote back, "You're going to change the world with this. This is huge." He already understood Hitch's implications just the way I had when I'd seen that echelon in the sky.

These two engineers became my early team. They were attracted by my sense of purpose and values, and I made sure we kept our mission front and center. I told the story of how important our project was over and over. When HERE announced its redefined values, they aligned with our small team perfectly: *Be bold. Learn fast. Win together.* That we were all culturally aligned was no accident.

Two months after my talk, in August 2016, Mauri, Babu, and I gathered over breakfast to present our progress to HERE's CEO. As was my practice, each member of the team presented their own contributions *(seen, heard, valued)*. Edzard listened and then said, "Go build a prototype. You have ten weeks to do it."

Those amazing engineers were so inspired that they built that prototype in seven and a half weeks. It wasn't lost on any of us that we had built it using the methodology, values, and purpose of the platform itself: inspiring people in the organization to do great things by utilizing their skills on special projects outside their prescribed "day jobs."

These engineers who had just presented to the CEO of HERE were now making it possible for others like them to escape the narrow descriptions of their jobs and to experience personal and professional growth they ordinarily would have had to leave the company to achieve. This was a culture shift beyond anything previously possible—and now we would spread it to every single employee at HERE and then one day to the world. We came back to Edzard at that seven-and-a-half-week mark, and he blessed it for a pilot.

A FEW THINGS TO THINK ABOUT WHEN ASSEMBLING YOUR TEAM:

LEAN INTO YOUR SUPERPOWER

Don't talk yourself into leaving "soft" factors like compatibility out of your hiring. Founder Kathyrn Hanson of ALearn believes that women assemble better teams because they are "more sensitive to the fact that the team needs to work well together."

ENSURE YOUR TEAM MEMBERS COMPLEMENT YOUR SKILLSET

Culturora CEO and founder Jody Madala advises that, "The CEO's most important job is to build and support a team with complementary skills that can challenge each other's opinions and listen to each other's ideas with respect." She laughs about the fact that her CTO (chief technology officer) and co-founder is not only a tech superstar but also an influencer, with a huge TikTok following, two skills far outside her area of expertise.

CONSIDER INVESTORS TEAM MEMBERS, TOO

One founder counsels, "Don't just look for venture partners who would give you a check, but partners who would be there for you through the thick and thin."

POSSIBLE SETBACK:
Choosing the Wrong Compensation Model

SUPERPOWER:
Seeking the Win-Win

If I hadn't been on the inside developing Hitch, it would have been harder to identify an aligned team, but that doesn't mean it wouldn't have been possible. I believe that because of my constant evangelism, I would have found engineers in my network who aligned with my values—or they would have found me. If that had been my path, I would have had to consider the substantial risk my teammates were taking by devoting their time to the project. In entrepreneurship, compensation becomes an issue. Typically, for early-stage team members, there is a promise of ownership in the success. Did they get stock? How much? At what point? In the beginning, the terms are usually handshake agreements. This requires an enormous amount of trust. This is why, initially, garage start-up founders like Steve Jobs and Steve Wozniak are usually good friends with already-established relationships. That trust has to be strong enough to carry the project through phase one, after which formal agreements are necessary, even for friends.

In my case, I didn't own the IP, so I had no ownership to give. Being the CHRO, however, gave me the ability to become my team's powerful advocate. I fought to make sure that when performance management conversations came around, their leaders knew they were contributing to the company beyond their current roles. To their managers, I always brought it back to the core values of HERE that they were living. I also was always sure to give recognition. For example, whenever I could, I asked my team members to present to the board, to travel to important conferences, or to tell their story in an internal publication. My initial team members either went on to a change in role or remit or followed me on the entire journey when we spun out Hitch.

Being constantly thoughtful about compensation from the start isn't an aside. It's a fundamental issue that needs to be addressed early on, or it can come back to cause trouble.

POSSIBLE SETBACK:
Thinking Too Narrowly about the Message

SUPERPOWER:
Identifying the WIFM (What's in It for Me)

When you're acting out of abundance, not competition, you're always looking for the win-win, even when you frame your strategy. For us, the formula was simple: Hitch had to be a win for the company and for the employees. I knew that incorporating skills data and personal aspirations for growth into online employee profiles required an exchange of value. People wouldn't be vulnerable with their dreams without getting something in return. That exchange was going to be a talent marketplace. In a marketplace, there are buyers and sellers. In this case, there were project owners and project seekers, and we were going to digitally put them together using AI to match skills and aspirations to work.

The WIFM (What's in It for Me) for the employees was that they had new opportunities to build their reputations and to learn new things. They had a mechanism through which to be seen, heard, and valued. The company won because it could tap existing capacity, cross-pollinate across the organization, save money, and attain higher levels of productivity and output. Those could be innovation, new products, or improving existing products. There always had to be a balance between the outcomes.

When developing your WIFM strategy, remember to think big, beyond the obvious stakeholders. Managing partner Nancy Pfund and her venture firm DBL Partners did this with The RealReal, a designer used clothing site. She says:

> We saw very early on in that company's life that while it was a great shopping site, a lot of women worked there, and it

was very supportive to women, that it was also a sustainability story. Selling used clothing and buying used clothing was part of the circular economy, which was a term that was just starting to be used. We helped The RealReal develop a whole way to quantify the environmental benefits of clothing reuse over buying new clothing and calculate the benefits. Now, it's very commonplace for people to think that buying used clothing is better for the climate than buying new. But that wasn't widely understood at the time. And so The RealReal became a pioneer in the space, which helped when the company went public as the first circular economy IPO. At the time, it was a win on all sides—for us, for the company, for the investors, for the consumers, and for the environment.

Facing My Moment of Truth

Even when you exercise all your superpowers to avoid the setbacks you can control, there will always be issues outside of your control that will bring you to your moment of truth. When my mother was in the police academy, there was an obstacle course she had to get through. If she couldn't, she was done. Part of that course had a 6-feet wall she had to get over. She was struggling with it so much, her brother built a replica of the wall in our backyard, and she practiced constantly. She also failed constantly, getting very bruised and beaten up in the process. When the final test came, all the cadets—mostly men twenty years younger than her—cheered her on. She got over that wall.

I would think about that wall every time I wanted to quit. Whenever I wanted to say that I couldn't do something—that I was a woman, that the idea isn't good enough, that I wasn't good enough—I told myself that I had to fight through. My mother did a really hard thing. I could do a really hard thing. I could find my way over this. It was going to take some practice. I was probably not going to succeed every single time. But when the moment came, I was going to get over that hurdle.

When our team had our MVP (Minimum Viable Product) ready to test, it was time to take it out into the world—or, in our case, out into the company. Although we knew it was a great idea on paper and it looked great in POC (Proof of Concept), now I had to get leaders to use it. No matter what your idea is—new software or a new process—you're asking people to do things differently, and that's a huge challenge. We built a plan to take the software to two business units so that they could share talent across their organizational boundaries. Our first step was to sell it to these leaders.

I'll discuss the considerable hurdles we faced at this stage in detail in chapter 4, but for now, I'll just say that not everybody was all in. Some in my own organization were the worst critics. If I didn't have my own organization behind me, I would be sunk. You can't be a one-woman band. Wherever I looked, there was opposition. Sometimes, it felt minor. Other times, I would think, *well, this is the moment of truth. This hurdle is too high. Do I have it in me to continue to fight for this project?*

I had enough leadership experience by now to know that reaching a hurdle is not a point at which you stop—it's where you accelerate. If you stop, you're done. I wasn't ready to be done. I had to lean into my superpowers: abundance mindset, collaboration, purpose, values, teambuilding, WIFM, and my win-win message.

Thus, when it came time for my moment of truth, when I was facing so much internal opposition to Hitch, the answer was always to continue. I had set a solid foundation in my business and my life based on my superpowers, and they always guided me to a workable solution.

The Joys of Fighting Through

Winning usually looks like throwing your hands in the air while the crowd cheers. That, of course, is pretty darn cool. But for most founders, they're not after recognition or adulation or even trophies. Instead, something deep inside has moved them. They created a movement, a category, or changed people's lives. If your mission is to change the world in some way, when you realize that mission, it's up there with other major milestones in your life like graduating from college or getting married. It's pretty phenomenal and deeply personal. You owe it to yourself and to the world to push through the obstacles. The world needs your idea. Take the time to set a stable foundation early on for your journey based on your superpowers, and you'll be prepared to face your moment of truth. The reward is worth the effort.

> You owe it to yourself and to the world to push through the obstacles. The world needs your idea.

Being Sure the Conditions Are Right

One of the biggest decisions facing early-stage entrepreneurs is whether to embrace intra- or entrepreneurship. Both choices hold their own potential pitfalls and rewards. I urge founders to take the time to consider both journeys. I chose intrapreneurship, and it led to eventual entrepreneurship. Others take the opposite journey. And still others, choose one or the other and stick with it. For female founders, which choice is right depends on complicated factors, some of which men don't have to face. The next chapter explores the intrapreneurial world to help you determine if that's the place your idea might thrive.

LESSONS FROM FEMALE FOUNDERS
Early-Stage Setbacks

> Even if you're happy, if you're working on something that drives you that day—there are still going to be bad days. There are going to be bad months. Sometimes there are bad years. But things change and you can pivot, and things work out at the end of it.
>
> —KELLY RYAN BAILEY, GLOBAL SILLS EVAN-GELIST AND FOUNDER, SKILLS BABY

> Co-founding a company with the wrong person is like those moments when you first start dating the wrong person. You know that there are red flags, your friends are telling you there are red flags, but you ignore them. You say, "But I'm having a good time." And you are. During the honeymoon phase, it's amazing.
>
> —ANONYMOUS FOUNDER

You don't need a hundred customers on day one, you need one. Then you just work with that one customer and just get to know them better and grow with them, grow within them. Eventually, customer number two will come along, and you start the learning process all over again.

—JODY MADALA, CEO AND FOUNDER, CULTURORA

I had my first big customer meeting with Hewlett Packard on September 11, 2001—which of course was the day of the attacks on the World Trade Center in New York City. It was surreal. I had a one-year-old and a five-year-old, which put everything in perspective for me. HP had employees in New York, and that was devastating. I remember being there with my husband, looking at the TV, and thinking, *am I still attending this meeting*? Everything that had seemed so important just moments before suddenly didn't feel so important.

**—BARBARA FAGAN, CEO AND FOUNDER,
ROI COMMUNICATIONS**

Chapter 4

ORGANIZATIONAL ANTIBODIES AND THE SWIM UPSTREAM

NAVIGATING THE WATERS OF INTRAPRENEURSHIP

> *I felt like I was one of those Olympic hurdlers who kept catching my back foot and being knocked to the ground, until I decided to take the next hurdle by simply walking around it.*
>
> **—DENISE HUMMEL ISAACSON, J.D., FOUNDER AND CEO, REVWORK.AI**

Denise Hummel Isaacson, J.D., spent the majority of her career as a lawyer, desperately wanting to extricate herself from that litigious environment. As she wasn't trained to do anything else and had no intention of re-educating herself in an alternative profession, she decided to leverage her background, come up with a great "big new idea," and launch into entrepreneurship. She told me:

> My idea, which while somewhat commonplace today, did not exist when I developed it, was to create a cross-cultural business model that would leverage the differences in culture for strategic advantage. I was not interested in creating something that was based on understanding cultural norms with an eye to not making embarrassing mistakes. I wanted to create a methodology that would upskill professionals and businesses with a global mindset that was focused on the business objectives they sought to achieve.
>
> The idea took off and within a short period of time, my company was conducting trainings for Fortune 200 companies in the U.S. and abroad. I knew to scale the business, I would need funding to invest in digital technology. I also knew that female founders rarely got the funding they needed. I knocked on every door, pitched to Angels and Venture Capital. Every time I got close, the door ultimately slammed.
>
> I began to feel that the world of entrepreneurship might not be open to me, or at least not open at this place and this time, but before accepting one last knockdown, I decided to see if I could side-step the barriers to funding and grow my business inside a more established one.
>
> That is just what happened. One of the largest consulting companies in the world decided that given enough resources and tools, I could likely scale internally at their company, which I didn't have the ability to do externally. They had a

physical and staffing presence in every developed nation. They had an unsurpassed innovation and technology budget, and there were other great minds that could complement my ideas and execution.

Sometimes, we need to side-step around a hurdle, instead of leaping gracefully over it. There is no shame in it and the success of the outcome is no less sweet. We do, however, need to approach all business endeavors with caution. As women, in particular, being given a seat at the table does not mean that we are given a voice. We must negotiate and plan for not only the economic remuneration proof-points, but the human interaction proof-points before we take advantage of an intrapreneurship opportunity.

Hummel Isaacson urges women who are considering intrapreneurship to ask themselves the following questions:

- How often and with what velocity do women rise within the organization?

- What is the specific budget for my innovation, annually?

- What staffing and level of staffing will I have?

- How will my performance be evaluated?

- How are my peers and colleagues incentivized to help me rather than compete with me internally?

- What strategic internal stakeholders will I be introduced to?

- How will I be supported in obtaining customer relationships and other revenue opportunities to help me succeed?

Her intrapreneurship experience was priceless once she returned to the entrepreneurial world. She had learned so much about technology and big business and had met incredible big thinkers and colleagues in her network that ultimately led to her significant business success.

The cautionary tale, she warns,

is that without proof points on these critical questions above, before I arrived in my intrapreneurial home, a lot went wrong once I landed there. I was not invited to critical internal meetings. I was not introduced to critical customers and prospects. My performance was evaluated in arenas where I had no control over the outcome. My ability to scale my idea was limited by inadequate resources and staff.

There were also intangible things she experienced in her intrapreneurial environment that she was not prepared for. For example, she had always valued her "go-getting" assertiveness, a quality that her male colleagues found "unlikeable" and said so. She coped by changing the tone of her voice, using a disarming lilt and a passive glance, so that she would not be perceived as a threat. The need to be less or different from her own true self did not serve her or her new home very well. Whether entrepreneur or intrapreneur, as Hummel Isaacson puts it, "the light, the spark, the insatiable drive to succeed cannot stay alive in darkness."

> Whether entrepreneur or intrapreneur, as Hummel Isaacson puts it, "the light, the spark, the insatiable drive to succeed cannot stay alive in darkness."

Going Inside: Considering Intrapreneurship

Adriana Gascoigne said, "Intrapreneurship is the gateway drug for entrepreneurship." And, her words may be especially true for women. When female founders are faced with the bleak statistic of only being able to capture 2 percent of all venture capital, it may feel as if intrapreneurship is an easier choice. Often, it not only carries less risk but is also strategically sound. But as you can see from the aforementioned example, while intrapreneurship can offer huge benefits, it also holds hidden dangers. An environment that seems perfect on the face can hold hidden traps, while an environment that might feel all wrong on the surface can hold the key to success. In this chapter, we'll discuss how to recognize the inevitable organizational antibodies that exist inside companies, how to assess which you can successfully overcome, and then how to do it by using your "female" superpowers.

> "Intrapreneurship is the gateway drug for entrepreneurship."

POTENTIAL ANTIBODY:
Toxic Culture

KEY TO SURVIVAL:
Knowing Your Authentic Self

In the aforementioned example, Hummel Isaacson knew that where she worked was "the epitome of the old boys' network" and that she "was not a person who could back slap and be out on the golf course."

But she hadn't fully understood until she was inside just how powerful that network was and how she would be perceived as a threat for daring to proudly stand outside it. Holding onto her authenticity proved to be harder than she anticipated. Often, strong women entrepreneurs encounter this problem because what has worked for them in the past stops working in the wrong environment. The antibodies come out, intent on throwing out the "invader."

Inside this company, she did not, as she put it, "fit the persona." The bias was often unconscious, spreading to even the women in the company who didn't support her. She told me, "There are two types of women in business. The women that climb the ladder and pull others up after them and the women who climb the ladder and then pull the ladder up after them."

> "There are two types of women in business. The women that climb the ladder and pull others up after them and the women who climb the ladder and then pull the ladder up after them."

At her company, she often encountered the latter.

"There were very few women that assisted or supported me in any way … [they operated] largely from a point of view of scarcity; there were only going to be a limited number of women that were going to make it."

When they looked at her, they only saw competition.

It's important to note that despite the company not being a fit, her intrapreneurial journey wasn't in vain. First, she grew her product, which she was passionate about. Going inside, she knew, benefited thousands of people she wouldn't have been able to reach otherwise. Also, she learned skills inside that helped her in her future entrepreneurial endeavors, including seeking venture capital. At the time of this writing, she's had three successful entrepreneurial exits. She believes that her success came in part from having learned that one must embrace authenticity but with a caveat.

Hummel Isaacson said,

> It is key to make a strong assessment of who the person across the table is, whether male or female and ask what one needs to do as a leader with objectives... In the end, the only person you can change is yourself.

She now counsels other female founders that "sometimes, it's necessary to dissipate any human dynamics that might be taking place, including intimidation." But when going into a long-term situation like intrapreneurship, you must fully consider the culture of the institution in which you're throwing your hat. How long can you sustain being inauthentic for the purpose of reaching your goal? In the end, she felt she was paying too big a price for suppressing her values.

Ask yourself:

- *What is the existing company culture?* Talk to people already inside the organization to get a sense of what's ahead.

- *What values will you not compromise on? Will standing up for those values make survival impossible inside the organization?*

- *Do you have any power to change the culture or is it too strong?*

- *Will changing the culture give you satisfaction, or will it be too high a personal price to pay?*

- *Can you find a way to negotiate ownership of your IP so that if the culture isn't a fit, you have an exit strategy?*

POTENTIAL ANTIBODY:
Leadership's Resistance to Change

KEY TO SURVIVAL:
Prove and Communicate the FOMO (Fear of Missing Out)

Although I also faced a great deal of resistance, my own intrapreneurial journey was quite different from the story mentioned previously. Unlike Hummel Isaacson in the previous example, I wasn't in a toxic culture. In fact, the culture at HERE was as good as I could have wished for. And yet, I still had to fight an uphill battle. When you're an entrepreneur, starting from scratch, you can erect your own organization. As an intrapreneur, the organization is fully constructed and working for a lot of people. I was taking that structure away, and people naturally weren't sure that was such a good idea. Change is hard for everybody, especially leadership.

Once you decide on intrapreneurship, it doesn't matter if you are in semiconductors or software or manufacturing; industry leaders are not incentivized to change. In my case, I had to convince people to share their talent across business units. Most organizations operate under a scarcity mindset and organizational constraints. In fact, leaders are purposely given constraints because that's how corporations get things done. Now I was going to go out and tell them, "Yes, you're responsible to get your work done, but you're going to share your talent with other parts of the organization, too." It just didn't make sense to many leaders.

Sure enough, when Hitch was ready to test, we ran a change readiness assessment and found that our biggest hurdle was going to be getting senior leadership inside HERE behind it. We had to convince them that if they shared their talent, they'd still get the work done for which they were accountable. If a German division borrowed an engineer from France, the French leader had to see that her engineer was gaining leadership skills that he could bring back to France and meeting a German network of talented engineers that the French division might need next month. And perhaps, most important, the French engineer was happier in his job because he was being noticed and appreciated internationally, using his talents and skills. It was win-win for everyone involved.

I didn't understand, at first, just how tough that message was going to be. I basically had to convince leaders to change the way they were doing things. They weren't bad people or even bad leaders. In fact, they were excellent at what they did. In a way, this was the problem: why should they change if things were going so well? I was threatening their knowledge base, their jobs, their expertise, and what was comfortable to them in their day-to-day work life.

The first key was to start slow. As I mentioned in the previous chapter, we started the move to this new paradigm with a voluntary pilot program within two of our engineering business units. We ran it for ninety days, collecting data and tweaking systems. Talent from one business unit was being tapped to work on special projects in another business unit. In return, talent from one functional group was pulled into another functional team.

More projects were getting completed faster. Employees were happier and reported an intention to stay longer in their jobs, cementing their loyalty to the company. And, crucially, everyone was still getting their "day jobs" done because they were motivated to use that 40 percent of themselves that was not engaged in their current role, the capacity that had been lying dormant, just waiting for an opportunity to shine. The rollout was so successful that the CEO gave the green light to roll it out company-wide.

For many, the results weren't far from the fairy tale that my engineer Mauri Niininen had described in his email. It was thrilling. We were changing lives at HERE and getting projects completed faster and with greater efficiency. I'd be in an all-hands-in meeting in Berlin or Chicago, and employees would stand up and give testimonials.

They'd say, "Thank you for building this platform. I would never have been able to experiment in this type of career had it not been for this tool." Or "My team would never have solved this customer escalation without this." Or "I'm in Germany, and I wouldn't have ever known that an engineer in Berkeley could solve our problem if it weren't for this platform."

It was extraordinary. Never as a CHRO would I be thanked for HR software—ever. So much unsolicited praise was coming in, it felt downright bizarre. My team and I were in heaven. We had a dream lab of 8,500 people in fifty-five countries from various functional units and cultures in which we got to test our concept, de-risk it, and figure out what was working and what wasn't in a closed environment. That was a huge advantage—the magic of intrapreneurship.

And yet, despite our success, going up against the existing corporate structure still wasn't easy. It was like asking leaders to write with their left hand when they're right-handed. It was really tough. I would preach to them that you get what you give. I was telling company leaders,

When you give people choices by opening the operating model and saying, *you can spend ten percent of your time over there*, suddenly you're tapping all this discretionary effort and engagement that they were just not giving. Watch! You won't lose anything. Let's try it and see.

The enthusiasm wasn't deafening. But I knew that once leaders began to see success in other divisions, it would become viral. All leaders have a FOMO. My thesis was that if I was able to show success in two organizations, other leaders would be afraid that they were missing out on too much talent because they were unable to tap the entire enterprise. Now they wouldn't just have twenty-five people in their headcount. They'd have the entire capacity of a global company at their fingertips. It was a competitive advantage. They'd think, *I gotta get on this*. That human nature was the psychology that I leaned into. Leaders have an incentive to get work done. They want to do it at as low cost as they can. They want to get it done as fast as they can with high quality, and they don't want to lose people.

When I was able to show our success, other leaders began to hop onto the bandwagon, and we were happy to welcome them with open arms. All the talk in the world never would have convinced them. I had to prove change. But also, all the changes in the world wouldn't convince them; I needed to be there constantly, pointing out the results of what other leaders were doing.

Ask yourself:

- *Are you passionate enough about your idea to devote yourself nonstop to changing what others don't want to change? Do you have the creative leadership skills to get that done?*

- *Will you be able to produce countable metrics that show how your ideas benefit other leaders?*

POTENTIAL ANTIBODY:
Employees' Resistance to Change

KEY TO SURVIVAL:
Prove and Communicate the Win-Win

It isn't just leaders who are resistant to change. Employees within your organization also have to buy into your innovation. We had to convince people to offer up information about themselves to the whole internal network. For Hitch to work, employees had to give their data and be vulnerable and tell the world, *here are my aspirations, here is what I need to learn, here is how I want to grow, here is what my skills are.* We knew intuitively that people wouldn't try something new unless they understood the value. In order to overcome their perfectly valid objections, we needed to prove that this new way of working was win-win for everyone, not just the company but the employees, too.

I had to find ways to prove and communicate that value. I spent so much time and effort communicating the opportunities that would open up for employees to learn, to apprentice in a new field, or to share the skills they had that were lying dormant. The employees who tried our platform got access to opportunities to contribute on a broader basis, to learn new skills, to leverage what they already knew. When other employees saw their peers becoming engaged, promoted, and given opportunities to grow, they came on board, too.

Ask yourself:

- *What fears can you anticipate? How can you help people overcome those fears?*

- *Will everyone who you're asking to change benefit? If not, how can you restructure to build in rewards for all parties?*

LESSONS FROM FEMALE FOUNDERS
Intrapreneurship

When I was inside IBM, I was met with "No" and "we can't do that" all the time. It was just friction. At first, I accepted the friction. I was just willing to believe it was a slow, sluggish place. And then I had an epiphany. I realized this is just like in the beginning when you start a company. The first thing that happens when you have an idea is you go tell ten people, and nine-and-a-half of them tell you it's dumb. There's not a line of people waiting to embrace it. That's your job to get it embraced.

-DEIDRE PAKNAD, CEO AND CO-FOUNDER, WORKBOARD

I was asked by the CEO of EDS to lead the design, creation of EDS' consulting division. We had a lot of great success with this new group, Solutions Consulting. It was truly a collaborative effort, with a global team and an amazing leader, that allowed us to create a very strategic team for EDS. … I really liked that way of working because it was something new that I had so much fun doing.

**-SHEILA TALTON, CEO AND FOUNDER,
GRAY MATTER ANALYTICS**

How will you know whether you should take that leap from intra- to entre-? If you increasingly find yourself daydreaming about what it could mean to have more control in your career, you may be an entrepreneur. If you hate slowing down to match the pace of your company … if you're crazy resourceful, accustomed to getting shit done and taking charge, you might be an entrepreneur.

—ADRIANA GASCOIGNE, CEO AND
FOUNDER, GIRLS IN TECH

Chapter 5

INSIDE OUT

THE SPINOUT AND PREPARING FOR THE PITCH

> *You go girl! This solution is going to be a game changer!*
>
> **—DR. BEVERLY KAYE, CEO AND FOUNDER, BEV KAYE & CO.**

The first time I understood that we could earn revenue from Hitch was in April 2017 when I gave the closing keynote to the Society of Human Resource Management Strategy Forum in Miami. This was an audience made up mostly of CHROs. These were the people who own the HR strategy in their companies. I gave the closing keynote about the talent platform we had built at HERE. I explained how it changed the trajectory of our company by innovating on the operating model. I had screenshots of the platform, case studies, and even videos of our CEO talking about its strategic importance. When I went to the Q & A, Beverly Kaye, a career development guru and legend in the industry, stood up and told me how excited she was about the solution I had built. I couldn't have been more thrilled. She was someone I looked up to my whole career.

At the end of the keynote, CHROs lined up to talk to me. They asked, "How did you get the CEO to buy into this?" "How did you get the employees to share their data?"

They had so many smart questions that I had the answers for. Most important, they said, "There is no software like this. Where can we get it? Are you going to commercialize it?"

It turned out that I was, but in the long run, this would not play out as I thought. When I got back to work the following week, I spoke with my CEO, Edzard Overbeek, about the potential revenue-generating opportunity we had right in front of us. I explained to him that I believed commercializing the talent platform we developed at HERE, at this time formally named Hitch, could be a new source of revenue. Of course, Edzard's initial reaction was positive, but then he asked how I intended to go to market. I said, "I will sell into my own network of CHROs."

That is exactly how we did it. In 2018, we worked with our legal team at HERE to create a subsidiary of the company, which would operate under HERE North America as Hitch, Inc. and be sold internationally under Hitch, B.V. in the Netherlands. By early 2019, we had sold our first customer, Dolby Laboratories, and continued to close more customers. We were off to the races and began building out the team. In February 2020, I got on stage in Athens at our global sales conference in front of our entire sales organization and did the closing keynote. They were excited about the possibilities of what this product could do. It was something new. We had done it. We were going to make Hitch a viable, salable revenue source for HERE.

Just as we were preparing to ramp up Hitch with a stronger go-to-market engine and support from the HERE sales organization, the world took an unexpected turn. In March 2020, the COVID-19 pandemic hit, and it was unlike anything any of us had seen in our lifetimes. The world felt as if it was falling apart. Business as usual was no longer possible. At HERE, that meant focusing on their customers and business. On April 4, 2020, the board announced they were carving out all noncore businesses. That included Hitch.

> **COVID only made it more clear to me that the world needed Hitch now more than ever.**

I had to pivot—fast. HERE owned the IP. If I couldn't find a way to save it, it would be dead. I couldn't even develop a slightly different idea on my own because as a student of the market, I knew if I started over, I'd be too late. The market window had passed.

I couldn't let Hitch just die. Hitch represented six years of hard work and my dream of a revolutionary way of working that could improve countless lives and companies. COVID only made it more clear to me that the world needed Hitch now more than ever. I also couldn't let it go without me and the other HERE employees who had worked so hard to get us this far.

I proposed a spinout—forming Hitch into its own, independent company. The board agreed. They gave me time until June 30, 2020, to get funding and spin out, or Hitch was no more. This meant that I needed a term sheet in hand by June 1. I had fifty-eight days to do something I'd never done before: raise venture capital.

I had to mobilize an internal team to work on the spinout. I had to get a pitch deck together and start pitching like crazy for funding. Meanwhile, I had to run a 750-person operation in my newly appointed role as chief innovation officer at HERE. And all this in the middle of a pandemic. Nobody had any idea what was going on. Chaos and fear were rampant. I was in meetings every week about how to move forward, including Saturdays and Sundays. Added to this was that now beyond global human resources, I was running IT, quality management, program management, and innovation management—almost all new functions I'd never run in my career. I had to keep my finger on all that. I couldn't shortchange my day job at this critical moment, but I also couldn't let Hitch die.

The internal strife grew exponentially as everyone became more and more panicked by the expanding pandemic. What was going to happen next? No one had any idea. The executive team at HERE gave me their blessing to take my team with me; they were pleased to get their salaries off the payroll at this uncertain time. But I still had to convince my twenty-five people that leaving HERE with me to spin Hitch out was a good idea. My team was wondering, *is this a good time to take the plunge into a start-up?* My peers were becoming more and more hostile because they were thinking, *what about us? You're leaving us now?* Had I found a lifeboat and I was leaving them behind?

My family was also in a swirl as I had a son coming home early from college in Boston, two high school students, as well as our third-grade daughter, all in virtual classrooms at home. And yes, I learned very quickly two things—I wasn't smarter than a third grader *and* Maslow's Hierarchy of Needs now included Wi-Fi. Everything was turning inside out.

Venture firms themselves were in chaos. Pandemic restrictions meant no one could meet in person, so their operating model was broken. How was I even going to get people to meet with me? I was going from intrapreneur to entrepreneur in unimaginable conditions.

No one thought I could do it. The world was at a standstill. In my quiet moments, even I had my doubts.

The Reality of Doing Hard Things While Female: The Toll on Family

I had a lot of conversations with my husband during these times. We had a very atypical family. My husband stayed home with the kids from the time my third child was one year old. Without his commitment to the family, I would never have had the time or the space to commit myself to my job and to Hitch. But I was still a mom. I still needed to be a part of the family, especially during the pandemic. I had a role to play. It wasn't as if he could be both mom and dad.

I needed to check in with my own core values. *Am I really going to just drop everything other than this mission?* Maybe I should just do my day job and stop trying to do all this. I was running double time. I had a global organization to run and a family. Maybe it was a little much. My husband would say, "I want to encourage your dreams, but you've to check in with yourself every once in a while. This might be too much." He would come down in the middle of the night to find me in my office and ask me if I was OK. *What are you doing working so late? You need sleep!*

Did I? I was in the flow. I had to keep going. There were many times when my husband stepped up for me and many times when I had to let go of work so that I could focus on my family. There were times when a child was going through something or there was a happy milestone that needed attention at the exact moment I had an important business obligation. At those times, I diverted my attention to my family. If I didn't, I knew that I'd end up out of balance fast.

Losing my family was not an option. But losing Hitch wasn't a good outcome either.

Luckily, my husband and I had built our family around our partnership. We had a similar purpose and values based on an attitude of abundance and win-win. My husband was my partner at home just as my engineers were in the office; we were all on the same team. We were of like minds, both of us deeply committed to do whatever it took to build a win-win life. Because of our abundance mindset, we reminded each other that my giving to Hitch wasn't taking directly away from him and the family. It charged me up and gave me more energy and resources to devote to them. It wasn't a zero-sum game. With careful planning and understanding, there was enough of me to go around.

And so, I moved forward to get funding and spinout Hitch in fifty-eight days, the hardest thing I'd ever do in my career.

Getting Ownership
STRENGTH: ABUNDANCE MINDSET

Intrapreneurs, as opposed to entrepreneurs, have an extra step: getting (or retaining) ownership of their product.

Hopefully, as an intrapreneur, you're able to negotiate ownership of your IP before you go inside. But that's not always possible, as in my situation with Hitch. In the beginning of my intrapreneurial journey, before the spinout, I had tried to get clarity on my ownership position. The reality was that my CEO didn't have the power to help me, because it was the company, not him, that had invested in Hitch. Even if he wanted to help me, and I believe he did, the likelihood was slim. Part of me was a bit devastated by the thought of that. But my optimistic, abundance mindset told me, *where there's a will, there's a way.* I will figure it out. There is always a way. That is just the way I'm wired. I knew deep down that the way would present itself.

And amazingly, it did. Now that Hitch had to go, I needed to find another win-win-win, for myself, my team, and for HERE. Luckily, the years of external evangelism I had done nonstop for Hitch during my years at HERE paid off. We had independent firms come in and do an analysis of Hitch. They concluded that the value of the company was tied entirely to me. The board signed ownership of the company over to me to make the spinout more attractive to investors.

People ask me all the time, *how did you do that? I don't get it.* Getting an IP back and a hundred percent of the cap table in a spinout is very unusual. They just couldn't comprehend it and were incredulous. They'd say, "I never heard of that." Having a clean cap table just made the funding process that much easier, so I was quite fortunate to have jumped that hurdle.

I believe that I was able to achieve this because of that win-win mentality—finding a way to have both HERE and Hitch win in this equation. I also believe that there were a lot of people who just didn't think I could really make a "go" at this, given the likelihood of failure in start-ups was so high. That being said, I leveraged that abundance mindset with a little bit of fearless confidence that we could do it. This was my strength and the strength of so many women.

And I was extremely lucky with the timing of the pandemic. If that hadn't happened, my story may have ended differently. Don't be afraid to take advantage of the lucky break. As my husband always said, "You need to position yourself for opportunity so when the time comes, you're ready to take advantage of it."

I was set—ready to do the hardest thing I'd ever done in my business life. I was ready to launch.

Learning to Pitch
STRENGTH: WILLINGNESS TO LEARN

No matter where you are in your journey, start learning to pitch now. I had started learning and practicing pitching to investors before the pandemic when I was on the path to spin out Hitch as a subsidiary of HERE. Because I had been in learning mode before I was in desperation mode, I had a head start that became invaluable.

> **Don't be afraid to own what you don't know and to extend your network beyond what you don't know.**

Don't be afraid to own what you don't know and to extend your network beyond what you don't know. For years, I had been reading books, scouring the internet, studying pitch decks, and watching videos. In addition, I asked my "personal board of directors" for advice and then asked them for introductions to other founders to get more advice. I'd ask, "Do you know anyone that I should talk to?" I literally interviewed everyone I could about the process. I asked how they approached the pitch deck. What did they put in it? What did they learn from their conversations with VCs? What were the formulas they were looking for? Did they have sample pitch decks they could share? I studied other people's successes and failures ad nauseam. Weekends, nights, and mornings, I was out there meeting people for coffee, digging for information. My former CTO at HERE Technologies was a serial entrepreneur. I asked him about getting funded. *What was that like? What were your agreements? How did you do everything from the inception to close?*

One good friend and a female VC, Cathy Chiu, sat with me over several coffee chats in the Valley to teach me the models of how they evaluate companies and evaluate founders. She told me, "They can like your idea, but not like you. They can like you but not your idea. Or they can like you and your idea, but no matter what, they each have their own formulas for how they invest." I took copious notes in three different two-hour sessions with her. And then, I would go back to her and ask her questions. I can't emphasize enough how important those meetings were.

I talked to people in venture who were investors. I talked to a lot of founders. I talked to leaders of various funds. I talked to a guy who did a spin in at Cisco and then spun out. I talked to lawyers who were friends. How would I structure compensation? What should I expect? I went to everyone in my network I could to learn as fast as I possibly could, both big picture and small detail. One example of a small tip that helped enormously was the "Rude FAQ" that came from my good friend and serial entrepreneur, Brian Lent. This meant that I'd sit down with my team and brainstorm every difficult question VCs could ask, no matter how outlandish. We'd write out the responses, every nitty-gritty question that scared the crap out of us. Then we'd decide who would jump in to answer when it came up in a meeting. This became priceless in more pitches than I could count.

My friend Judy O'Brien was one of the partners at King & Spaulding. She was smart and had seen a lot. She took me under her wing and was my guardian angel, trying to help me figure out how I should be thinking about an agreement for myself, how I could build a board or my own guiding coalition that was independent, feeding me financial advice that I didn't have. She taught me about corporate structure and financial acumen around venture.

I was a powerful C-suite executive—but I was also a humble, constant student. You have to be intellectually curious. You can't just say, *I'm going to do something I've never done before, and I'm just going to throw myself at it.* You have to be smart. You have to make yourself a student of the process, which is exactly what I always did when I took on something really scary. I threw myself into it. But I always did it in a smart way. I would find people who had done it before and learn from them.

Celebrate Small Wins
STRENGTH: FORMING ALLIANCES

Every time I went out to pitch, I was determined to learn from that, too, and incorporate that learning into the next pitch. Before the pandemic, I was doing as many practice pitches as I could, learning as I went from my mistakes. As founder Mackenzie Branigan advises,

> Take as many meetings as you can and ideally start with the least important ones upfront because you just get so much better by the end. You can start to anticipate every single question you're going to get, answer them preemptively, have slides prepared, see which pieces of your pitch aren't working and where you need to tweak it.

I would ask people for "friendlies," meaning that I wasn't really pitching them for funding but more for feedback. I had a really great early pitch with a prominent firm that had made a lot of investments in workplace technology. There was a woman on the VC team, and I thought, *here's a woman in venture. She's going to get me.* I did really well on the pitch; however, I learned that I was too early for them.

Now, when I went back, I knew exactly what they needed to see. I was much more confident, and the pitch was better. It went really well. It felt like a supportive environment, and the woman on the team was excited about what I was doing and very interested.

They didn't fund me.

But that female VC became a contact. We had formed a relationship. She

Every swing can't be a home run, but it's progress.

started to invite me to other events with female founders. She helped me grow my network. This led to more connections and more learning and more pitches. Every swing can't be a home run, but it's progress, and I chose to recognize that and let it raise me up.

Another time, I got a chance to do a practice pitch to Uri Levine, the founder of Waze and a recent board member at HERE Technologies. I asked Uri if he would hear my pitch and give me some feedback. It was maybe 2018, so very early on. I wasn't out for funding; I just wanted his unabated feedback. He sat down with me and a few of my colleagues in a conference room in Amsterdam. We demoed an early version of our product, and we walked him through our pitch. He was blown away. He had some small feedback, but at the end, he said,

> Kelley, this is really great. This is going to change the world. You're going to have to spin this out at some point because it's noncore to HERE. Are you ready to go from being an executive in a big company to an entrepreneur? It means a lot of sacrifices. This cushy executive job goes away. You will have to ask yourself if you are really ready for that.

That felt like such a badge of honor for someone like Uri Levine to say we were going to change the world with our technology. His validation and perspective carried me through numerous disappointments and doubts that were to come. Priceless.

Is Venture for You?
STRENGTH: CREATIVITY

A lot of people don't want to go for venture capital, and that's always an option to consider. To them, that's like selling your soul to the devil. In some ways, it can be. With venture, you get validation; you have access to their portfolio and their ability to make connections for you. But you also run the risk of losing control. As you'll see in chapter 9, that happened to me. There's no going back. Once you take that first dollar from venture capital, you can't turn around and say, "Oh, I'm going to set my own expectations for growth." You're in.

Still, I am satisfied with the path I took. I was not going to bootstrap my company and put my family at risk. I was also not going to ask my friends and family for money. To me, that was too much pressure. Thus, the only option I had outside of venture were Angels. These were experienced investors—some who knew me personally and others who didn't. In fact, the Angels who invested in me were all experienced female investors, and one of them, Judy O'Brien, former Partner at Wilson Sonsini Goodrich Rosati, P.C., was also on that personal board of directors I mentioned prior.

It's a personal choice. What's important is to go into it with your eyes wide open. There is no golden parachute when you mortgage your house, and you take everything out on credit cards. Smart founders take smart risks. They don't take no risk. What is smart for you may not be smart for the next person. Only you can make those choices, and only you have to live with the consequences—good or bad.

Lessons from Female Founders on the Spinout and Preparing to Pitch

Educate yourself to the maximum extent possible. Not just what you can acquire in the public domain or even in terms of formal degrees. Have the foresight and the humility to speak to people who have succeeded and those who have failed, and leverage as much of that information as possible to upskill your own preparedness.

—DENISE HUMMEL ISAACSON, J.D.,
FOUNDER AND CEO, REVWORK.AI

I'm pleased that we're able to continue to grow at a pace that's comfortable for us, that allows us to make sure first and foremost that we're adding value to our customers and our buyers and differentiating in the market. And it's a huge learning process, so I think the worst thing we could have done is had a ton of money and just build something that we're iterating on still. So, I think we're exactly where we're supposed to be.

—JODY MADALA, CEO AND FOUNDER, CULTURORA

Chapter 6

THE PITCH

> *Fundraising can be very, very challenging, very demoralizing and humbling. And so, you need to have your passion and your belief in your company established before you go after that capital.*
>
> **—JODY MADALA, CEO AND FOUNDER, CULTURORA**

Early on in the pitching process, I pitched to a very well-known venture capital firm in the Valley. Afterward, one of the male partners took me aside and told me that being a woman was going to make it very difficult for me to get funding. He advised that I might want to consider putting some more men on my team in leadership roles. He was just trying to give me the straight scoop, to help me, but regardless, I was insulted. I wanted to have a lot of women on my team because I strongly wanted women to help one another. This was a way to practice what I preached. These were my values. I walked away from that meeting furious, calling many of my former trusted colleagues, complaining that this was unfair and that the bar was much higher for me. Some of those women told me, "You need to go back at it." They were harsh with me. They said, "He's right."

I really started to think about what they said. He was just being honest; having a mostly female team was a disadvantage. There is so much unconscious bias that even if a firm is not intentionally discriminating, it's made up of human beings who have bias. There's the way we want the world to be and then the way it is. We see it in the data. Forty percent of business owners are female,[11] and yet

- the percentage of venture money in the United States won by all-female-founder teams has never gone over 3 percent;

- in 2022, all-female-founded start-ups raised 1.9 percent of US venture capital, down from 2.4 percent in 2021, and the lowest percentage since 2016; and

- if a male is added to the founder team, the percentage of venture "skyrockets" to 17.2 percent, a trend that "has remained consistent for at least a decade."[12]

In other words, it's not just harder for women to raise venture funding—it's a lot harder. I see it every day in the women I mentor and in the stories my friends and colleagues tell. I never added a man to my team just to please the venture firms, and yet at times while pitching, I had men on my team because they were an integral part of

---

11   Lisa Jucca, "Female entrepreneurs' glass ceiling is intact," Reuters, March 8, 2023, https://www.reuters.com/article/us-womens-day-breakingviews-idDEKBN2VA0UF.

12   Dominic-Madori Davis, "Women-founded startups raised 1.9% of all VC funds in 2022, a drop from 2021," Tech-Crunch, January 18, 2023, https://techcrunch.com/2023/01/18/women-founded-startups-raised-1-9-of-all-vc-funds-in-2022-a-drop-from-2021/.

Hitch. My experience lined up with the numbers: when I had a male CTO, I raised money. When I had an all-female team, despite our proven success and growth in the marketplace, we weren't as successful in raising venture capital.

Allison Baum Gates, a general partner at SemperVirens Venture Capital, explains it this way:

> Obviously, it's horrible and we can do better, and we should do better. My hypothesis has always been that, especially when it comes to early-stage funding, investing in start-ups is incredibly risky. You're writing a check for something that is very likely going to be worth nothing. Really at the early stage, you're investing in a founding team. And I think that disadvantages women for two reasons. One is that VCs are pattern-matchers and so they look at what has worked before, and they look for people that have had that same experience. When it comes to founders, that means investing in second-time founders. A very common prerequisite for many funds is that they only want to invest in founders who have built big, successful companies before. That's obviously a self-fulfilling prophecy when it comes to female founders who aren't getting funding and therefore never get the opportunity.
>
> Also, when you're in a highly risky situation, you're trying to predict the behavior of the founder. It is inherently easier to predict the behavior of people that are like us because we know how we think. With somebody from the same life experience, the same educational background, the same network, it's much easier to predict what they would do and what they're capable of doing given they have a shared

network. So that means we need more female VCs to invest in more female founders. Over 90% of venture dollars are controlled by white men.

Miriam Rivera, CEO, co-founder, and managing director at Ulu Ventures, agrees. She says,

> What I realized is that guys network and get support from other white males automatically. Those older men see themselves in these younger guys. It is easier to fund people that look like you and you can relate to. It is why the numbers are what they are.

So what is a female founder to do? First, get ready for a tough ride. Then, use your strengths—your unique point of view—to your advantage so that being a woman becomes your greatest strength.

The Emotional Toll of Doing Hard Things

Once you start pitching, you need to prepare yourself for the emotions that come with playing a low-odds game. Failing wears us down, no matter how strong we think we are. I made over forty pitches before I got one "yes." That was a lot of rejection. It wasn't easy. Playing in an unjust world causes stress, and that stress takes its toll.

Everyone has their own, personal source of inspiration, an outside, invisible force that helps them when things get tough. You need to find this inspiration. Money and success are not going to be enough. Pitching is too hard. We all have moments when we worry that we're not capable of achieving something. We feel insecure. We face imposter syndrome. Or we're just really, really tired and struggling while we see men sailing through with what seems like half the effort. This is the moment when we need to reach outside ourselves.

Getting funded is harder for women. It just is. There is bias. The bar is higher. But I urge you to do it anyway. That is a theme in my life, and I want it to become a theme in your life, too, or you won't make it. One 2022 study found that 29 percent of women believed that they couldn't get access to capital and thus were less likely to try.[13] If you're one of those women, I urge you to find the inspiration to try anyway.

What will get you through hard times?

My mom was the fire underneath me. There's an old song that seems to magically come on the radio just when I need it: Mariah Carey's "Hero." I don't really believe in magic, but if I was having a fight with a friend, a challenging time with a child, or trouble at work, that song would always come on. That was the song they played at her funeral. For me, it was a reminder that I wasn't walking this path alone. She was my guardian angel.

My mother's story was that she went against the odds. By becoming a female police officer in 1994 at forty-four years old, she did something that was considered next to impossible. Despite incredible struggle, she achieved it, and she paved the way for a lot of others behind her. She lost her life doing that, but she also became a codified hero for what she did for other women, for women her age, and for women who wanted a second act and didn't want to be defined by what they've done before or by how others see them. She knew she could be a better detective, that she could do it really well with empathy, by bringing the "female" skills that were missing from that world, even though everybody said that it wasn't needed and would not happen.

---

13   Bank of America, "2022 Women & minority business owner spotlight," 6, https://newsroom.bankofamerica.com/content/dam/newsroom/docs/2022/Women%20+%20Minority%20Business%20Owner%20Spotlight%20ADA.pdf.

I wasn't going to let those voices—both internal and external—stop me, and I don't want them to stop you either. I want them to inspire you. I was going to give pitching my all for myself, my family, my team, the millions of people in the workforce who needed a new model of work—and I was also going to do it for other women just the way my mother did a generation before. The only way we won't continue to be defined by what we've achieved previously, or by what others see when they look at us, is to keep on fighting and doing the thing they (and the data) say we can't do. When I was pitching Hitch, I didn't have a sister, and I didn't have a mom anymore. At my hardest moments I'd think, *those would be really nice things to have—other women who know how hard it is and who believe in me and my ability to fight through anyway.*

I believe in you. So do all the other women who need you to do this. We are out there—other women walking this path with you. We know how hard it is. We acknowledge your struggle because we've been there. When you decide to take the leap into the unknown, when things get hard, reach for whatever deep, inner inspiration moves you, and then keep going. You're doing more than getting your company funded. You're literally changing the world for other women coming after you, and you're joining the tribe of the women who came before you. Let that inspire you to keep going and to not doubt the value of the sometimes very unfair struggle you're about to undertake.

Focusing on What You Can Control

I've probably pitched a hundred times and learned a few things along the way. The most important is to be prepared:

1. Study prior investments that the fund has made.

2. Understand the formulas that each individual fund uses to make investment decisions: the general formulas for pre-seed investment, seed investment, Series A, Series B, and so on.

3. Look up the people who are in the firm and their backgrounds. Do they have a strong background that would make them an expert or help you if they were to be on your board?

4. Make sure you have clear roles for the pitch meetings. What role is the CEO going to play versus your CTO?

5. Learn how to execute a pitch in fifteen to twenty minutes so that there are ten minutes left for questions.

6. Remember that you're interviewing them as much as they're interviewing you. You're marrying these people. Due diligence is key.

7. Venture funds are looking for an indication of product market fit. If you don't have any signs of traction, in their minds, they're investing in on a promise. When you're a concept and you don't have customers or revenue, you might be too early.

8. Know your business model and financials cold. You can't farm this out to your chief financial officer (CFO) or director of finance. This may be the one time to show the level of business acumen you have. This is especially true if you're the engineering, marketing, or sales genius and finance is not

your expertise. This is also especially true if you're a woman, and there's inherent bias against you.

9. Ask yourself who you want calling you in the middle of the night when something goes wrong. Do you want an investor who's going to coach you through it, who will be there for you standing behind you and supporting you as a founder? Or is it just money?

Who to Pitch?

Pitching likely means facing sitting across the table from men. In 2022, while most venture capital firms had a 50/50 gender split at the lower levels, 95.5 percent of US VC firms still had majority-male general partners—and general partners are the ones who ultimately write the checks. Women in US VC firms still make up only 16.1 percent of all general partners.[14] Allison Baum Gates explains:

> The way venture capital funds operate is that in order to become a general partner, meaning you're actually making investment decisions and you have dollars to deploy, you need a track record of investments that's over 10 years long where you've actually returned money to your investors. Getting to that point is really challenging, especially if you don't have money to deploy yourself. So in the call for diversity, venture funds' answer was to hire women, young women, who are junior. But what I see time and time again is that those women are not empowered internally. They're

---

14   PitchBook, "All in: Female founders in the US VC ecosystem," 2022, p. 8 and 20, https://pitchbook.com/news/ reports/2022-all-in-female-founders-in-the-us-vc-ecosystem.

not able to actually deploy capital, and their voices are often silenced in investment committee meetings that are largely dominated by older, experienced men. So there are so many existing barriers. While it's a lot easier now for a woman to break into venture, I think it's maybe even harder than ever before to actually succeed and get to a place of power.

The conversations that I've had with a lot of female founders is they feel really disappointed and disillusioned that female investors are not putting their necks out and working harder to make investments in them. The challenge is a lot of these female investors are not in a position where they can really do that. But because of how venture works, they would never tell you that because then they'd stop getting access to great investments in the first place. So it's a really challenging dynamic, and part of my goal is to help educate female founders on how venture funds work so that they don't waste their time barking up a tree that is never going to bear fruit.

This disparity at the check-writing level leads many female founders to seek funding from female-focused venture funds. Currently 4.5 percent of venture firms boast a female-majority group of decision makers.[15] Many of these firms talk the talk of diversity and the desire to support women.

One thing that's very important to understand about pitching is not to take anything at face value. Many female founders advise others to seek female funders, myself included. But sometimes, this isn't the best path. There are always going to be good and bad actors everywhere. You can't assume that every woman VC is a friend simply because their credo is about supporting female founders.

---

15   Ibid., 9.

Picking an investor might feel a little like dating. Everyone is on their best behavior during courting, and only later does the real person show up. Do your vetting. You are essentially "getting hitched" (yes, pun intended) to these people. Do they have good character? What has their track record been with other founders? They may not always be who they claim to be. Unfortunately, some of the founders I spoke to were more disappointed by the women than the men because they put them too high on a pedestal. Because of this, they just had further to fall.

Adriana Gascoigne, founder and CEO of Girls in Tech and author of *Tech Boss Lady*, advises, "Find a partner, not a manipulator … talk to other founders … do a bit of amateur investigating … Are they honest? Do they come through with what they say? Who is angry with them or super happy with them?"[16]

"Seek out independent evidence that they are collaborators, not manipulators," founder and CEO Denise Hummel Isaacson, J.D., of RevWork.AI advised. She specifically credits speaking with another female founder before she invested with one venture firm, causing her to include specific terms in her contract that she hadn't considered.

Hummel Isaacson said,

> I did not have my usual attorney goggles on because many of the VCs were women. I spoke to another female founder who alerted me not to bank on their gender affiliation as a proof point. Had she not told me to be careful, I would not have had the caution to put certain legal safeguards into place when drafting the funding documents, which is what saved me when the relationship went south.

Another important thing to consider when getting funding from women-centered venture firms (albeit incredibly disappointing) is that getting your first round of venture from women may hurt you in later rounds. Researchers Isabelle Solal and Kaisa Snellman wrote in the *Harvard Business Review*:

> We analyzed more than 2,000 venture-backed firms in the United States and found that women-led firms whose first round of VC funding was raised exclusively from female VC partners were two times less likely than those whose first round included male partners to eventually raise a second round. No matter the size of the initial funding round, the industry, the geographic location, or the prestige of the investor, female founders were consistently less likely to close a second round if their first round only included women. Conversely, for male-led firms, the genders of the first-round investors had no impact on their ability to attract future investment.[17]

The authors interviewed one investor who advised, "It's almost like, you'd want to do the hard thing first, and get a few men brought in."[18] To this, I advise that like all things, you need to do what's best for you in your individual situation. Understand the research, evaluate your options, and proceed with your values front and center. We all can't change the world with every action, but we all can do the best we can when we can.

---

17   Isabelle Solal and Kaisa Snellman, "For female founders, only fundraising from female VCs comes at a cost," Harvard Business Review, February 1, 2023, https://hbr.org/2023/02/for-female-founders-only-fundraising-from-female-vcs-comes-at-a-cost.

18   Ibid.

Focusing on What You Can't Control

When you're pitching, you may experience overt sexism, harassment, racism, or inappropriate questions, so you need to think beforehand about how you'll respond. These are ways that some of the female founders I've spoken to have dealt with pitching situations they've encountered:

ON INAPPROPRIATE QUESTIONS AROUND MOTHERHOOD

Sally Thornton, CEO and Founder, Forshay:

How will you do it all? Who will take care of your children?

Sometimes potential investors ask these questions out loud. Other times, it's just an uncomfortable feeling in the room when, for example, they see a pregnant founder. In the end, it doesn't matter because either way, they still vote with their dollars. So what do you do?

Sometimes we think about negotiation as just a win. How do you win the money? How do you win the negotiation? But you need to think about what you are winning. Sometimes, you don't want money from people who doubt your ability to be a mother and a founder, and it's best to walk away and count it as a win because you don't necessarily want to deal with that kind of person.

But if you get those kinds of questions or that sort of energy from a potential investor who you think is someone that can actually be influenced, you might want to persevere. You want to move them into exploration mode and not defensive mode. If you feel defensive, you're in the wrong partnership. If you feel like this person is open to co-creating with you, then explore it and try to negotiate. Negotiation, as defined by Maggie Neely at Stanford Business School, is about all sides winning.

It's not a win-lose. I don't think you have to attack and champion women's rights or be a warrior because then you're in battle. No one wants to be in battle. If they're a curious person with a growth mindset who is open to new ideas, you want to meet them where they are. Maybe they're just genuinely curious as to how you can be a mother and founder. They just haven't seen it yet, seen the perspective you bring to the table. Their fears are based on old social science norms that you need to counter. In this case, you want to ask questions, to activate their prefrontal cortex and get them away from fear.

A person can't be scared and curious at the same time. You can say, "Are you asking if I'm going to be a dedicated leader? Do you want to know how I'm going to handle maternity leave?" And then have that discussion.

ON OVERT SEXUAL HARASSMENT

Janine Yancey, CEO and Founder, Emtrain:

I've been a mentor at Techstars, so I've been there to help and support female entrepreneurs in the Techstar ecosystem. I've heard a lot of shared experiences where the pitch becomes an excuse for an investor to literally hit on the woman entrepreneur. It's pretty frequent. I tell my mentees to be super clear that they're not interested in having those types of conversations. They're interested in having a business conversation. If they feel it has gone beyond the pale, I tell the woman that she should contact Techstars because Techstars needs to know which investors in its ecosystem are not good collaborators. And then, you just move on. You don't spend time. When you're pitching, you're talking to forty, fifty, sixty people. It's a lot of work. It's a lot of time. So you don't have time, and harassers are basically wasting your time. Not to mention how offensive it is.

ON RACISM

Sheila Talton, CEO and Founder, Gray Matter Analytics:

I don't have specific stories about encountering discrimination in pitching, because it's all of them, every one of them. I'm not white, and I'm not male. So there you go. And I'm seventy years old. So, put that on top of it. But I'm at a point in my career that I can say what's on my mind. Now I say, "Tell me a little bit about your fund," and they start talking to me.

Then, I say, "I got on your website and the only women I saw were one in marketing and one in HR."

So they try to explain and I say, "Talk to me about people of color." They say, "Well, we have a mission and we're trying to find people out of grad school and bring them up."

To that I say, "That's what everybody says, but you don't seem to be making progress at that." I'm not trying to be hurtful or spiteful. I tell them, "It is about progress, and it's not going to ever happen if you keep doing the same things that you've been doing and expect a different result."

But things are starting to change—slowly. One African American male entrepreneur called me last week. He's gotten his company up to 12 million now, and the private equity guys are knocking on his door. He said, "Sheila, I get on their website. Everybody's white. They're all male."

He says, "Why would I want to give up part of my company to them?"

Anybody that knows me knows that I am highly invested in females and highly invested in people of color because it's just not been a level playing field, and it still isn't. I have raised around $30 million and the majority of my investors are African American and after that, women. Had I not had three African Americans in particular who make up my largest shareholder group, I wouldn't be in business.

Getting the Win

As I kept at it, I got better. I became smarter and more targeted about who I was pitching. I'd look at all the investors who had funded HR technology in their portfolios and target them with one-pagers. Sometimes I got the meeting; sometimes I didn't. I was going up to bat a lot, and there were a lot of strikeouts, a few foul balls, but not a single hit—until, suddenly, there was.

The magic of pitching is that while you ideally want more than one term sheet, all you need to get started is the *right one*.

For me, my one was Bill Elmore, who was an icon in the Valley. He was the founder of Foundation Capital in Palo Alto, a Stanford guy. Richard (Rick) Mirabile, whom I had known for decades, introduced us. Rick was one of my mentors in the organization development space. He was the founder of Success Factor Systems, which got bought by SAP and later blew up. He loved my idea for Hitch and had listened to me rant about it for years. One of his investors early on had been Foundation Capital. Bill had recently started his own VC firm with his son, Will, called Handshake Ventures. I sent Bill a copy of my first book, and he agreed to meet. Because of the pandemic, we met on the Stanford campus and, abiding by social distancing, walked and talked.

He got to know me over several meetings. At first, I was pitching him on me. I told him why I wanted to do this and what type of leader I was. Then, we got into the intricacies of Hitch.

All the learning, practice, connections, networking, and hard work paid off. After several weeks of rejections, I got a single, signed term sheet from Handshake Ventures on June 1, 2020. The effort had been Herculean. Almost impossible. It was a nail-biter. But with not a day to spare, we had pulled it off. We had the first round of funding we needed. We were ready to take Hitch out into the great, big world.

On July 1, 2020, it was final—signed, sealed, and delivered. Hitch had become a female-founded venture-backed company, and it was one of the most exhilarating days of my life.

LESSONS FROM FEMALE FOUNDERS
Pitching for the Win

One particular investor basically offered me the same valuation for a Series A as for my seed. He had devalued my company based on me being a woman and being married to my co-founder. I think he honestly thought he was trying to help me. He was very warm and friendly and huggy. I didn't need hugs. I needed money.

—DEIDRE PAKNAD, CO-FOUNDER AND CEO, WORKBOARD

There was one competitive bid where having gender diversity on the pitch team was one of the reasons we were chosen. So, when you're pitching to people or organizations that actually care about these issues, the fact that you're competing against a sea of white men in suits is not necessarily an advantage.

**—DENISE HUMMEL ISAACSON, J.D.,
FOUNDER AND CEO, REVWORK.AI**

Be proud and don't be afraid to shoot for the stars and have it understood that you mean business and that you can do audacious things. That might mean letting go of a more traditional, modest approach.

But if that isn't authentic, if you can't do that, then don't do it because you don't want this to be forced. Just try to push yourself to be a little bit more promotional. We want to see the grit, the commitment, the excitement that you have in whatever it is you're creating because that's going to get you through. It's not about counting the numbers or establishing a certain growth rate on the table in your deck; those numbers will change many times before you are through.

—NANCY PFUND, FOUNDER AND MANAGING
PARTNER, DBL PARTNERS

There are some amazing VCs and I am really looking forward to finding them. The same way I build relationships with customers and companies, I want to do that with the investor side because I don't think companies should look for money just for the sake of money. Look at investors as partners. Would you bring them on as a co-founder? Because that's literally what you are doing. And that's really the role they should take. They should not be people you're scared of.

—JODY MADALA, CEO AND FOUNDER, CULTURORA

Chapter 7

FLYING SOLO

NAVIGATING THE POST-FUNDING PHASE

> *"Embrace what you don't know, especially in the beginning, because what you don't know can become your greatest asset. It ensures that you will absolutely be doing things different from everybody else."*
>
> **— SARA BLAKELY, FOUNDER OF SPANX[19]**

I woke up on July 1, 2020, and thought, *I have the capital to get going and need to make it last.* My gift is my ability to be creative and unconstrained. Now, the pressure was on to manage cash, one of the most important parts of being a start-up CEO. When I was an executive with 750 people who worked for me, somehow that had felt more specifically like the company's responsibility and not mine.

---

19   Carl Potak, "122 Startup Quotes from High-Level Founders & Leaders," startupdevkit.com, October 9, 2023, https://startupdevkit.com/startup-quotes-from-successful-founders/.

Now, every day I was directly responsible for twenty-five people and their families all over the world. These employees had walked away from an 8,500-person, stable tech company to work for me. That was an awesome responsibility. It was all me. If I made a bad decision, I could be harming so many people's lives.

As I detailed in chapter 1, I didn't grow up with a lot of money. My parents were very middle class, often stressed about their finances. That anxiety was deep in my psyche. By becoming a CEO of a startup, cash preservation was now my biggest priority and thus a daily stressor. I had put myself into post-traumatic stress disorder (PTSD) mode. I would wake up at 3'o clock in the morning, feeling as if someone was standing on my chest. All of a sudden, I felt as if I was back to living hand to mouth. At times, I was in actual physical pain. The anxiety surprised me. I had been dealing with impossible situations for decades, and I'd always found a way. I knew I'd find a way through this, too. But I wasn't mentally prepared for just how hard that would be.

Every decision from that day forward carried with it the weight of this new responsibility. Now, I understand that no matter how much success I had in the past, running a venture-backed company was unlike anything I'd done before. For me, the first unexpected challenge was my emotional stress over having to think about money all the time.

My wiring made it hard for me to deal with money. Your wiring may light up danger signs in other areas—maybe fear of failure, imposter syndrome, or family issues. Or maybe stress won't be your issue at all, but instead, you'll have to face unexpected outside forces, such as an economic downturn or a new, powerful competitor in the market. Maybe, you'll find out you're pregnant—or that despite trying, you're not. Whatever your challenge is, know that it will come, and you'll need to meet it head-on and devise a strategy to overcome it. When you're the boss, there's no one above you to make the final decisions. It's all on your shoulders.

Of course, being on your own is also wonderful. Despite those 3 am moments, I had never been happier in my career. There are wonderful upsides to being out on your own, and it's important to celebrate those, too. You've worked too hard for this to not enjoy your success. Now that Hitch had spun out and was funded, I was on cloud nine. Here I was, evangelizing my message that there was a new way to work. I truly felt Hitch was changing the world one company at a time, and I took every opportunity to enjoy the ride. Even some of those early mornings, I still struggled with the reality of "the buck stops with me."

Overcoming Stress

Doing hard things day after day, week after week, year after year will expose your vulnerabilities. In fact, if you're not feeling overwhelmed as a founder, you're probably doing something wrong. But one super-power of being a female founder is our compassion and empathy for ourselves and those around us.

Stress shows up differently for everyone. Founder Denise Brouder would go to work in the early days of her company, SWAY, sit at her desk, put her head on her computer, and cry. And then the next day, she'd do it all over again.

She says,

> I was consumed with self-doubt about how well I was doing. I had such conflict between the desire to achieve the financial goals I set and a desire that was more meaningful,

social, and purposeful. In those early days of SWAY, I was really at odds with it.

Looking back, Brouder sees that what was standing between her and the success that she desired was her own self-doubt. Once she let it go, things started to happen for her and for SWAY.

CEO and founder of Wellist, Ashley Reid, discovered that her stress showed up as not being able to sleep. She found herself "sucked into a 24/7 Wellist world." She explains,

> It's very easy for me to stay up till all hours, staring into my inbox. It took a long time for me to realize that was a stress response and getting eight hours of sleep was more important than answering emails. I actually need every hour of rest.

Now, she puts sleep first, avoiding the late nights and the extra anxiety that losing sleep triggers. Reid says she's learned that her body is giving her signals. When she felt that anxiety in her twenties and thirties, she "felt like it was deeply personal to me."

Now, when she feels that bodily reaction of "there's something brewing in me," she tries to see it from an outside perspective. She'll tell herself, "That's just my body giving me information that I have to do something differently." Now, she recognizes it as part of the job—something that happens to everyone and that has to be dealt with as urgently as a customer deadline or a presentation to her board.

For founder and CEO Adriana Gascoigne of Girls in Tech, her first sign of stress was discovering that her hair was falling out. When she went to the doctor, he recognized it right away as a classic physiological stress response. She responded by doubling down and pushing through. Looking back, she saw that she needed better coping mechanisms. Now, she sets boundaries by blocking time in her schedule for "me-time," just the way she would for any other important meeting.

To me, stress showed itself as a whiplash between high highs and low lows. I was either cranking on all cylinders or shut down. There was definitely no in-between. To live in a black-and-white world like that is painful because the whiplash can be debilitating. I was either praising myself or beating myself up. I couldn't find the Goldilocks just-right balance. It didn't help that I knew there was an upside to my anxiety. Anxiety had served me well because when I needed to dig into twelve hours of work to meet a deadline, I knew I could always just power through. I'd done that ever since I was a little kid.

But the downside is that once the project was done, I still couldn't let go. I held onto the stress like a pit bull. And then I got more exhausted, and it eventually caught up with me. Learning to let go of the stress and find that middle ground allowed me to be a better CEO. Now I and my family recognize the signs that I'm falling back into my old black-and-white pattern. When we see it, we all speak up and pitch in to be sure I get back to a more balanced life.

The good news is companies, especially ones led by women, are starting to acknowledge that stress is a work-related issue that needs to be dealt with like any other. Barbara Fagan, CEO and founder of ROI Communications, says,

> The speech I give to new employees is the most important thing in your life is you and your own health because, without it, you can't do anything. And second is your family and your loved ones, including your pets. And if either of those are not in order, attend to those first and we support you 100% no matter what. Work comes third.

TO DEAL WITH STRESS:

ACKNOWLEDGE YOUR ANXIETY WITHOUT JUDGMENT

It's not good or bad; it's a signal that something needs to change.

TALK ABOUT YOUR STRESS

The more we normalize anxiety, the more everyone can see it's not a personal problem but a systemic one. Not seeing anxiety as a personal failure allows us to deal with it rationally.

RECOGNIZE YOUR OWN PERSONAL TRIGGERS SO THAT YOU CAN LEARN HOW TO WORK AROUND THEM

Often, our anxieties are deeply rooted in childhood trauma. Uncovering that trauma may be the only way to make a plan to move forward.

DON'T GO IT ALONE

Just as there are experts in finance and marketing, there are experts in stress. Bringing in a personal coach to help you should be as easy a decision as bringing any professional onto your team.

The Bias of Being the Boss

When a woman steps into the role of being a founder, she's stepping into that role of CEO, of field general. The bias comes out and you need to be prepared.

—JANINE YANCEY, CEO AND FOUNDER, EMTRAIN

Emtrain, founded by Janine Yancey, provides harassment and bias training in the workplace. In that capacity, Yancey often goes inside companies to talk to employees. When she speaks with women in their early thirties, they often tell her that there are no issues with any kind of bias. Then, she talks to those women's female bosses, usually in their late forties or older, and they tell her, "Well, let them wait because they will see it. They're not there yet."

Same company, different experience. Yancey explains,

> You're suddenly not seen as competitive because you're throwing your hat in the ring for a non-workhorse job. You're trying to get a more senior role, and it doesn't happen. In the land of founders, that translates into you not going for your seed money anymore. You're going for the bigger money. The lesson is don't expect things to get better. Actually, things might keep getting harder. There's more scrutiny, more critique, and more bias.

To counter the opposition to your change in role, first, you need to expect it. Like any outside force, you can only control how you react, and how you do that depends on your specific situation. Founder Kathryn Hanson advises that the best way female founders can react to bias is to help others. She's seen that when we help one another get into senior leadership or entrepreneurial roles and then succeed in them, the stereotypes lose their power.

Hanson says, "If you face opposition to your views, you shouldn't be surprised. You need to expect it. Just like with any kind of opposition, you can only control how you react, and how you do that depends on your specific situation." She also says, "I've been on boards where I'm the only woman in the room, and those can be challenging. I've also been on boards where there were three women out of ten, and those were joyful, lovely boards." Making the world a more welcoming place for other women shatters the stereotype and brings support where and when women need it most: at the top.

Setting a Realistic Pace

The early days can feel like an emotional roller coaster. One day, you sign a huge new customer. The next day, an investor rejects you. It's a constant up and down. You must apply the same principles and use the same muscle that got you through all those first-round pitches to get your original term sheets to keep going. Keeping everyone behind you inspired is your number one job, and raising more money is the primary way to do that. You have to keep on getting back out there every day, no matter what happened the day before. That's what entrepreneurship is about.

> You have to keep on getting back out there every day, no matter what happened the day before. That's what entrepreneurship is about.

I had gotten a few million in cash and few more in a convertible note with some less favorable terms, including interest that would increase if I didn't pay things off on time. Taking the risk and getting that note saved my bacon later, but in the beginning, it only caused more stress. I had taken the note because I knew I couldn't operate on just the cash. It wasn't as if I was operating out of a garage or even just in North America—Hitch was a global start-up, with all the complexities that entailed. I was determined to make it work. I had an abundance mindset in all other areas. I had to consciously develop that same mindset around money. Fast.

After the last sip of celebratory champagne, the reality set in that I was at the helm of this company that is now venture-backed with so many dials to watch while also raising as much money as fast as I could. It wasn't just about being an inspirational leader anymore. I was going to have to be an operational leader as well. I had wanted to be a CEO by the time I turned fifty, and I had done it. But now I realized that the treadmill never goes to zero. I was at least jogging the entire time. It wasn't going to stop–especially the fundraising. No one really told me that fundraising is something you have to do every day, every week, every month of every year. I was a long-distance runner most of my life, so I knew about endurance. And yet, I came out of the blocks at a sprint. I started working crazy hours. My personal board of directors kept telling me, *This is a marathon. You can't sprint the whole way. You're going to have to set a pace that you can keep.* But that was hard for me because I was really excited, inspired—and scared.

To slow it down, I took a lot of walks. I had a team and customers all over the world, and no one could meet in person because of the COVID-19 pandemic. I would get up early and do my one-on-ones while walking. That stabilized my mental health until the lockdowns eased.

By now, I had pitched a lot of investors, so I had figured out their formulas. I started working with my lead investor to pitch his network. I was pitching at least two to three times a week on average. The pitch was constantly refined. It had to evolve as we evolved. Maybe we had closed another customer or maybe something had changed in the market. I had to rework the financials over and over. We were lucky because the pandemic created a huge tailwind behind us. Our technology was needed now more than ever because so many companies were now working fully remotely or with a hybrid model. They were forced to think differently about their operations, and we were there, prepared to help.

But while our technology was compelling, we were still early-stage. I hired a male CTO with a history of start-ups and really leaned into his experience. But with a female CEO, the bar was so high; we still got rejected a lot. I started to develop that thick skin, with calluses. I expected that out of ten pitches, only two to three would move to a second meeting. That meant that I had to fill the pipeline with a lot of investors. It felt as if 80 percent of my job was fundraising, which I didn't expect. I was excited to run my company, to spend time with customers and pitching the product. The customer facing role was important—I couldn't be everywhere.

For years, I was on stage all day long pitching to either customers or investors, then having to go back to the team to incorporate my learnings from every single one into the next one. It was key to prove ourselves by getting more customers. Revenue, of course, could provide operating capital and solve our funding issues. But I knew we couldn't depend on one or the other. I had to swing for the fences on both sides. That's true for all venture-backed companies, a rule of the start-up world. You need to keep getting bigger. The more you can grow your ARR (annual recurring revenue), the more you can secure additional funding, so the most important thing I could do was to grow revenue. But it's hard to grow revenue without funding to build the team and the product.

It was like being back in caveman days. I had to hunt and bring food back constantly—more than we needed because a famine might be coming, and we had to prepare. When you're constantly worried, instead of being excited about working with your customers and selling your product, you're preparing for whatever may be coming.

JODY MADALA, CEO AND FOUNDER, CULTURORA, ON SLOWING DOWN THE RIDE:

Madala purposefully started her company with a small team. She knew that she was expected to get customers and show traction really fast. But she resisted the pull as much as she could.

She said,

> I think sometimes that kind of fast growth is a negative because people realistically don't move that way. It puts start-ups in awkward positions where people are faking data because they feel like they have to show really fast, big growth too soon. It's not real. It's not organic. It's not the way humans think and work. Even start-ups don't always move that fast to try something new. Companies need to grow thoughtfully, otherwise, they can find themselves in very uncomfortable situations.

By not taking venture money and keeping her team small and agile, she was able to let Culturora grow at a pace that was comfortable for them. I wasn't in that position with Hitch. We had to keep moving at the pace venture expected.

Putting Values First

Despite the pressure to keep growing, pitching, and selling, the good news is that now that you're the boss, you can put your values front and center while you do it. You're in charge, so ask yourself: *What are you doing to help other women? What are you doing to increase equity overall? What did you learn from your journey so far that you want to change?* Now is the time to stick to your guns.

For example, Denise Hummel Isaacson, J.D., founder and CEO of RevWork.AI, points out,

> The priority of Diversity & Inclusion will always be marginalized in a down economy. In hard times, CEOs are focused almost entirely on increasing revenue and decreasing costs. At that juncture, it's not easy to convince most CEOs that different points of view will bring more innovation and revenue sources and shake up the homogeneity that allows risk to propagate. If you're the CEO, you can practice diversity and inclusion in all markets, up or down. You can lead the way forward.

As Hummel Isaacson puts it, "At the end of the day, we can never change anybody but ourselves, but if enough of us do just that, we can create the momentum that changes our little corner of the world."

Ashley Reid is another founder who leads from values. She says, "Investors have come to me with economic propositions over the years and they say, 'We'll take care of you, but screw over the other guy.' I can't say screw over the other guy. They don't understand how my decision-making works."

I found the same phenomenon with Hitch. Investors have asked me, "Do you want to be rich? Do you want to be queen of the future of work?" Sure, at times I'd think about how nice it would be to have taken that route and gotten the fast, easy money. But for me, my passion to create a workplace that worked for everyone was always front and center. As much as I had to constantly seek funding to stay alive, I wasn't in it personally for the money. I was in it to prove that Hitch could change the world.

Founders and Families

Early in her career, Miriam Rivera, CEO, co-founder, and managing director of Ulu Ventures, co-founded a start-up with her husband. When they were raising their Series B, one of their investors told them that they didn't want a husband-and-wife team, let alone a co-founder who just had a child. Rivera told me that he explained it wasn't because it was necessarily bad for the company, but it wasn't in the best interest of the children. Rivera reflects, "Clearly this was a bias. One of my first encounters with such a bias."

What she took away from the encounter was that being a mother is what made her a good leader. She says,

> Motherhood taught me that I can't waste time on things that don't matter to the business and to focus on the important things that made us grow. It helped as a filter and pushed me to focus on the things that were strategic for the company.

Serial entrepreneur, intrapreneur, and advisor, Kelly Ryan Bailey, founder of Skills Baby, found that it was the corporate world that didn't work for her. Being a founder gave her a "return on her investment from a time perspective," a way to get where she wanted to be professionally without the commute and other negative aspects of corporate life. She said, "I wanted to have choices and freedom that were not available in the corporate world as a working mother. Some of my businesses initially started as side hustles because I had to step out of the workforce multiple times."

As the mother of four, I understand the struggle. My husband left his work to care for our family while I was still an executive, so I had an unusual situation. And still, it wasn't easy. While I ran my global start-up, I still had a family of six. Sometimes, it felt like too much. Other times, my family was my source of inspiration to work harder than ever. If I had only Hitch in my life, I may not have survived the really hard times because my family gave me perspective.

DENISE BROUDER, FOUNDER, SWAY, ON BEING A MOTHER:

There is no divide of who you are. You don't have to choose a business or a baby. You can have both, but you have to define what that means. We have to redefine what we mean by hustle culture and work culture, and business building. Life has never been 9:00 to 5:00. It never will be. So, I don't think of it as such. Work isn't 9:00 to 5:00 either. I work at all odd times of the day when I feel energetic and when I feel creative, when I feel pulled to it. And then I spend time with my family when I need to. My whole company and existence in this sense is a social experiment. I am wondering for myself if I can be meaningfully involved in my children's lives and develop a meaningful business at the same time. But my whole business model is about promoting flexibility. If we can create a world of flexible work where we can be present in the parts of life that we need to be, we dissolve the only factor that will allow women to stop hitting the glass ceiling.

As a society, we need to redefine womanhood and motherhood. And it's not only because I feel disadvantaged. It's because economically, we need to do this. You are one person. You are living one life and endeavoring to make it count through the language of our work. Some of that work is paid work. Some of that work is unpaid. I'm always working at something. I might be working at resting. I might be working on a presentation. I might be working with my family. Our waking hours are one long stretch of work.

I don't think I'm one person at work and one person at home. I'm one person. I don't see a difference. I show up the same. These are my day clothes and my work clothes. This is my day hair and my work hair. This is my day voice and my work voice. I am only one person, in SWAY and in all parts of my life, and I found operating that way gives me a sense of ease. The world shifted around me once I changed my mindset. I didn't have to make a choice any longer. My choice is getting up and seeing it differently. That was my choice, and I had success with my family and success with my business.

The Joy of Founding

> I love the ability for decisions to be made really quickly. I love the excitement that comes with opening up a territory that no one else has ever known about, building a team that is your own team, and making the decisions. When you're working for a company, you're having to meet the company's mission, meet its revenue goals, and it's not on your clock, and it's not on your strategy. It's someone else's. And I think that having those things in your control makes what's hard much more fun.
>
> **—ANONYMOUS FEMALE FOUNDER**

From the stress to the bias to the constant pressure to raise money and stick to your values in a world that encourages winning at all costs, being out on your own can be a challenge. But it can also be wonderful. Those early days of Hitch were some of the hardest and most rewarding of my career.

Once the paperwork was signed and we were ready to fly solo, we had a virtual celebration with people all over the world. We opened bottles of champagne, and we celebrated our story: how we started, how we proved this concept of talent sharing, and how we were going to go change the world. We invited people who helped us with the spinout to that virtual celebration. Most founders will tell you that once you experience the thrill of being your own boss, it's hard to go back. I think there's a lot of truth to that. So allow yourself to feel the thrill. Don't let the good times roll by without patting yourself on the back for what you've achieved.

CELEBRATE

Throw a party for your team and your customers, or just go out to dinner with your spouse and kids. Include everyone in your celebration—or don't and go to a spa, sit back, and savor what you've accomplished.

SPREAD THE GOOD NEWS

Sharing your success on social media doesn't have to be self-centered. Talking about gratitude promotes loyalty of staff and team.

GIVE RECOGNITION

Now that you've made it, be sure to thank all the people who helped you along the way.

HELP OTHERS

No better way to celebrate your own success than to be sure others behind you have the same opportunity.

LESSONS FROM FEMALE FOUNDERS
Flying Solo

There's so much uncertainty in start-ups, but there's so much uncertainty period. So you might as well take the opportunity to pursue something that's fun, that makes a difference, that allows you to work with amazing, interesting people.

—JODY MADALA, CEO AND FOUNDER, CULTURORA

I believe in myself, and I bet on myself in the face of all kinds of adversity. I feel it's a sure bet.

—DENISE BROUDER, FOUNDER, SWAY

I would not have nearly been able to do the majority of things I've done if I have not learned it in the trenches of parenthood. I mean, if I can get three kids out the door with shoes on their feet, not flipping out, by a certain time in the morning, you put me in front of any board meeting and I'm fine. I know how to handle all those personalities because I deal with it day in and day out.

—KELLY RYAN BAILEY, FOUNDER, SKILLS BABY

Chapter 8

RIDING THE ROLLER COASTER

SURVIVING THE INEVITABLE UPS AND DOWNS OF ENTREPRENEURSHIP

> *My whole experience over the last five years building SWAY has been a daily struggle. It's been days of tears and crying. It's been days of joys and triumphs.*
>
> **—DENISE BROUDER, FOUNDER, SWAY**

Founder and CEO Jody Madala and her team started Culturora in October 2020 with a mission to help companies accelerate new-hire productivity and connection to company culture, especially for their Gen Z and Millennial workforces. When Culturora landed Home Depot as their first customer, they were shocked—and thrilled. From the outside, landing such a big first customer looks like an indication of a constant upward trajectory from day one. But the path from first contact with Home Depot to securing their business wasn't a straight line at all. In fact, some of the ups and downs were harrowing. Madala described the company's early days:

> We were just getting started whiteboarding our idea for Culturora, when I heard Ted Decker, Chief Operating Officer of Home Depot, speak at Carnegie Mellon. During the Q&A, I asked, "How are you thinking about culture during the pandemic and post-pandemic?"

> Those conversations laid the groundwork for an opportunity to reach out to him later. Nine times out of ten, those "reach-out-laters" fail. They fall on deaf ears. But for Ted Decker, they didn't. I was persistent. Not annoying, but persistent.

> After a couple of emails, he responded. He wrote, "What you're trying to do sounds interesting. Let me connect you to our head of HR."

Madala continued the conversation with HR. Culturora didn't have a product yet; they weren't trying to sell. They were trying to build relationships and get feedback to build the best product they could. HR eventually put Madala in touch with Home Depot's leaders in Talent, and she and her team began to see that the Talent space of organizations was where they wanted to operate.

At one meeting, Madala and her team came in to demo some ideas on a use case for entering interns to get feedback, and the woman in charge of that use case jumped. She said she was interested in piloting the product with their upcoming cohort of interns. Could using Culturora help acclimate them to company culture? Madala explains, "We said, 'Of course. Oh, that's wonderful. Thank you so much.' Then we got off the call with them, convened on a private video call, and said, 'Oh my gosh, we need to build a product—fast.'"

This was a huge opportunity. A great, unexpected high after months of exploratory work. They felt on top of the world. But they had to scramble. Madala told me, "The team worked hard to figure out the tech. But because we didn't have time, we had to use low-code technology."

When they started the live trial, things began to go wrong immediately. Madala said, "We were completely failing in front of Home Depot, which was not an awesome experience."

Our tech team was the most panicked as the demo continued to not work. They felt responsible for everything to work properly, and from their perspective, there was nothing anyone else could do. My technical team began apologizing. But Madala explained that this wasn't right in that kind of thinking: Jody assured her technical team by saying, "Never, ever apologize. We're all co-founders. We're all on this team together. It's not all on one person ever. I never want to hear an apology from anyone. We're a team. We all have the best intentions."

Madala recalls, "I said, 'We'll figure it out. We'll go talk to Home Depot, explain what's happening, and keep it calm there too.' Nobody panicked on our side or on theirs." In the end, "Home Depot understood. We fixed it. And then we moved on." Not long after, Home Depot became their first customer. In other words, the big high or the big low wasn't the end. It was all just part of the ride. How Culturora dealt with the twists and turns was what made the difference.

Enjoying the Ride

Sometimes as a founder, you look around and wonder how everyone else is having such an easy time of things. The secret is, they're not. They just hide it exactly the same way you try to. You feel that you can't look desperate to investors or to your employees, even if in the background, you're worried about cash or competition or demos that don't go the way you planned. The truth is that every single founder is in the same boat as you: figuring it out as they go

> **The truth is that every single founder is in the same boat as you: figuring it out as they go along.**

along. And while it's true that you don't want to appear desperate, there's nothing wrong with owning up to being human. Figuring out how you'll get up the next hill and then stay on top long enough before the next inevitable fall is just part of the process.

When Madala looks back on the trial, she doesn't remember it as a low point but rather as a chance for her team to learn and the relationship with the potential customer to deepen. So we failed in front of Home Depot. Was it bad? Yes. Was it the end of the world? No. Was it the end of our company? No. Did we end up stronger after? Yes: as a team, as a product, and in our relationship with Home Depot. That's really important. There are always down moments where things break, and the power is being able to stay calm.

Madala highlights another upside of the demo "failure." Once they fixed the glitch, they realized that they had built a successful, powerful product using low-code technology. Being forced to rush meant they could now avoid spending on high-cost engineering,

136

keeping their product costs low. In the end, Madala looks at the whole experience as a win that made the product, her company, and her team better.

REACTING TO SETBACKS:

REALIZE IT'S TEMPORARY

Every company goes through good times and bad.

LOOK AT EVERY EXPERIENCE AS A WIN

You learn something from every challenge.

ENJOY THE THRILL OF THE RIDE

Before founding Culturora, Madala overcame a life-threatening illness that shifted her mindset from valuing safety to enjoying risk. She explains, "I'm not saying you need to get as sick as I did to have that pivotal moment" where you realize "it's good to take chances because you never know."

Preparing for What You Can't Control

The COVID-19 pandemic forced a lot of founders onto what was often not just a roller coaster but also one gone out of control. The key to surviving the ride is maintaining stability and resilience in times of chaos. When done right, this can put companies on a better track than they were before the crisis. The key is being able to pivot with the new reality.

One female founder experienced this with the company she co-founded, a Software-as-a-Service (SaaS) platform with a focus on diversity, equity, and inclusion (DEI) events. When the pandemic hit, 90 percent of their customer pipeline was gone overnight. Not only were all in-person events suddenly canceled due to lockdowns, but a lot of DEI leaders were also fired or laid off from their jobs. She explains, "This made it really hard because those were the people we were selling to. We had to start thinking about other markets and areas of focus."

It wasn't easy. She says, "Not only was the world trying to figure out what the virus was, but also investors were still asking, *How are things going?* They still wanted to know how they were going to get their returns." Her company started having conversations around figuring out who their new customer was now that the world had fundamentally changed. They knew that HR was the hardest-hit department in a recession, so how could they make their product recession-proof? They were forced to confront the "things that are really hard, the things you can't control, the macro issues, and then figure out our strategy around those."

Instead of focusing on DEI leaders, they shifted to target general workplace program leaders who typically had budgets that were larger and more stable. In addition, they started thinking about the future of work, especially the pivot from in-person events to hybrid or online events.

"It was about forward projecting and thinking about how we could make our product future-proof. It was about reading what's coming, and also being prepared for things you couldn't see coming, like the pandemic, and then quickly pivoting." They were still on a mission around supporting DEI, but now by providing data to a broader range of programs, when the downturns came, they had a broader customer base.

Finding the Females

I had just experienced what was to date the high point of my career: becoming Hitch's CEO. What followed was months of meeting new prospective investors, learning and iterating, and pitching constantly, but we were still not getting new investors. Then, in December 2020, we were fortunate to have brought in How Women Invest, a female-centered firm with a mission to invest in female-founded companies. The due diligence process put us through the paces, and once we were through, I thought we were off to the races. We then brought on Broadway Angels and a few other female angels, including Judy O'Brien who was a member of my "personal board of directors." However, as successful as we were in closing female investors, finding male investors was still a challenge.

Still, with new investors on board, I was relieved. Now I had a bit more runway, and watching that monthly cash burn wasn't as stressful. We could spend a bit more on marketing, acquiring customers, and filling out the team. Still, this didn't mean that I stopped fundraising. Honestly, I thought it would get easier. I was wrong. There were still a lot more rejections from investors and customers than wins. I can't say for sure that it was biased, but in our case, only women investors were willing to take a risk on a woman CEO at the seed stage. If it wasn't for early female investors, I don't know if Hitch would have survived.

That was hard for me. I had been a pioneer in this market. I had established this category. But by the time I spun out Hitch from HERE Technologies, there were other players in the field that were very well-funded. My competitors were in B, C, and D rounds. Despite our wins, I knew we were falling further and further behind. Why would an investor take a risk on a small start-up when they could go with somebody further along in their journey?

Building a Big Brand

It was going to be an uphill climb, so as usual, I leaned into my strengths. First, I was going to build an amazing brand. Imagine you're walking alone on a trail, and you meet a mountain lion—what are you supposed to do? The answer is to look really, really big. The same principle goes for walking through the jungle of start-ups. It might just be you, you and your co-founder, or maybe a few engineers. If you don't have the funds to hire or you can't find the right people, you still have to show up big. When I met my competitors in the market, I needed to look like a company that matched their might.

> Imagine you're walking alone on a trail, and you meet a mountain lion—what are you supposed to do? The answer is to look really, really big.

Luckily, I had experience in branding. People thought we were a much bigger company than we were because of how the brand showed up. We were very professional from day one. Our logo, colors, and website were extremely polished and complete. For example, our navy blue signaled the IBMs of the world—the really stable, trusted, highly secure messaging. The green communicated innovative, fun, and fast-moving.

When it came down to our pitches, our demos, and our webinars, everything was meticulous in terms of the brand. We had our core values as a company, laid out and highlighted front and center to differentiate us from our competitors. We looked so much bigger than we were because who could have a brand like that with no money?

When customers or investors would meet us, they'd say, "I thought you were bigger." This almost always helped us, because if this was what we already looked like with just a small team and first-round funding, they could already imagine what we could do with more.

Leaning into Your Network

I had a background in journalism and as a communications professional, so not only did I know how to build a brand, but I myself could also be part of that brand because I was a thought leader in the future of work. I was credible. Our buying center was essentially human resource executives, and I was going to use that network however I could in a very grassroots fashion because we didn't have a lot of money to do anything else. People would take my calls and let me pitch them because either we were friends or they were peers in my network.

In addition, I put myself out there on webinars and panels. Because I was a practitioner, I was getting entry into the types of venues that vendors wouldn't get, such as CHRO forums. I had also just put out my first book, *The Inside Gig*, a thought leadership and strategy book. I was invited to give talks because I wasn't directly selling my product but instead selling the strategy, the systems, and the need for the technology.

Vision Is Everything

I had a broad vision of where we were going with the product well beyond where we were at the present time. I wasn't a software engineer or a UX designer, but I definitely had a vision—that was my strength.

I knew how I wanted it to feel and be used. We worked tirelessly on that vision with my very scrappy product team. I had been a practitioner for so many years, so I knew exactly what the holy grail looked like for other HR executives. They would say to me, "My God, if you could build that, we would be on board in a heartbeat."

Around the time we secured Broadway Angels, we closed a major global engineering and technology company based in Germany on a three-year contract with a two-year renewal. That was the lighthouse deal that launched Hitch. If this reputable, global company was willing to take a bet on us, we thought things were about to take off. *This was going to be amazing.*

The big lesson was that after the champagne, just like when we spun out or got our seed funding, I woke up the next day and thought, *we're twenty-five people, and we're standing up a 300,000-person, global organization.* That was going to be a lot of pressure. Instead of us standing on the shoulders of giants, the giant was now standing on our shoulders.

It was scary. But the team was super excited. We were going to learn so much through this very big, international customer. They were going to be co-design partners with us. We thought, *Oh my God, here we go. Strap yourself in. This is going to be a ride.* Everybody was super excited.

And yet, even though we had a huge customer, we still couldn't stop looking for funding because for the first year of the contract, it was going to be a slow ramp. Even though we sold a major deal, the revenue would be earned over three years. At any moment, the economy could tank, or they could say that we didn't deliver and wipe out their contract. The minute we sealed the deal, it was back to the grind. Looking back, taking on an enterprise giant, was a tall order. It was a lot of pressure on our tiny team.

Developing New Muscles

When you're an executive, you generally have a team of people underneath you who are specialized in running their operations. As a CEO, it's your job to set the vision and execute the strategy. When you take a step into the role of entrepreneur, you're forced to use different muscles. I was a great talent architect, great in front of customers, a great keynote speaker, and builder of a brand. But all of a sudden, I was using untrained muscles around finance, accounting, and tax. There were moments when it felt really uncomfortable.

I was constantly saying to myself, *How can I do this? I don't have the expertise in this.* But I had always risen to the occasion. I had always been a quick study because I found people who could be mentors. I kept on asking questions. I was a student of everything. Sure, I felt insecure at times. There were times I could have done better. But I always reflected on every experience, asking myself, *What did I learn?* Now I knew that the next time I had to talk to the tax guy, I would do better.

Still, we weren't bringing any other investors on board. Customers weren't closing fast enough. It was June 2021, and I and my investors were getting restless. I was starting to hear grumbling that it might be time to get a COO. I also wanted a COO, but cash was still constrained, and I wanted this to be someone who I felt would be a fit for the team and me.

I was more inclined to try to do it all than to pay another executive to come on board. But this decision wasn't all in my hands. My board and my investors had a major influence, and I was about to enter a new phase of being an entrepreneur: losing control of my own company—and I had no idea if this was going to be the end of my ride, a test of my endurance and compliance, or just another dip along the way.

LESSONS FROM FEMALE FOUNDERS
Riding the Roller Coaster

When you're an entrepreneur, you can't look too far into the future because if you did, you wouldn't be doing what you're doing. So you kind of just focus on today and a little bit of tomorrow.

—SHEILA TALTON, CEO AND FOUNDER,
GRAY MATTER ANALYTICS

I'm very conscious about how I show up as CEO. I don't see male CEOs, worrying about these sorts of issues. How they show up to their teams isn't a big issue for them. They're not thinking about it nearly as much as women CEOs because they haven't had the level of granular dissection.

—JANINE YANCEY, CEO AND FOUNDER, EMTRAIN

There is an expectation of trust with a Series A or a seed investor. That is the hardest stretch of a company's life. You cannot say all your doubts to your employees. Usually, you can't really say them to your partner either. That early investor should be a person that you can say all that to. And if they're good, they've seen it all, and they will help you through the doubt.

—DEIDRE PAKNAD, CEO AND CO-FOUNDER, WORKBOARD

I know many young women haven't experienced it yet, but I can tell you, with complete confidence, that it's not a matter of if, but when. The moment will come when you realize that the modern workplace, in every corner of the economy, is designed to make it spectacularly difficult for a woman to succeed. It's not so much that there's a glass ceiling at the end of our journey—it's that the entire journey is like navigating a glass minefield.

—LESLIE FEINZAIG, FOUNDER, FEMALE FOUNDERS ALLIANCE (NOW GRAHAM & WALKER)[20]

---

20   Leslie Feinzaig, "All I want for international women's day: No more female founder takedowns," FastCompany, March 23, 2023, https://www.fastcompany.com/90861837/international-womens-day-no-more-female-founder-takedowns.

Chapter 9

PIVOTS AND TRANSITIONS

MAKING MASSIVE SHIFTS AND COMING OUT STRONGER

> *You need to go for it and do it, and sometimes it's going to work, sometimes it's not going to work, so you try again. And that's part of the entrepreneurial journey. I don't think of it as a failure, but a step on the learning journey.*
>
> **—ANONYMOUS FOUNDER**

The female co-founder of a small, VC-backed start-up had gotten seed-round funding and was looking for the next round, but it was starting to become clear that some of their initial hypotheses weren't playing out the way that they thought they would. They weren't seeing demand take off in the way they had anticipated. Then COVID-19 hit, and the market shifted precariously. It became clear that the milestones they needed to hit were going to be even harder in this tougher environment.

The founder explained,

> We were in a position that we could keep going and continue to try to pivot and find something to save us. But a lot of the potential pivots were just not things that I personally believed in. I wasn't as excited about them. I couldn't see the big-picture vision.

As things continued to move in the wrong direction, she and her co-founder began to feel that it was "unrealistic that we'd be able to do what we needed to do to hit the next round with our current trajectory."

They decided to shut the business down. She told me,

> It was horrible. It was the hardest six months of my entire life. My whole life, this had been my dream, my goal. I'd worked so hard for so long to get there. So just for myself, it was really hard. But more importantly, I felt a deep sense of responsibility to our customers, vendors, investors—and to our team. One of my biggest priorities and biggest accomplishments as a founder has always been hiring amazing people and creating an amazing place to work, and now, I had to disappoint all those people.

The cliché of start-ups is that you should "fail fast and fail often," but that bravado often masks the reality of the pain and heartbreak of seeing your dream crumble. Failure is under-discussed in start-up literature, but it happens at some point to almost everyone. According to the Department of Labor Statistics, 70 percent of businesses won't survive five years, and first-time business owners have a five-year success rate of only 18 percent.[21]

Failure happens across all demographics, and yet women often take the hit harder, as many female founders feel a responsibility not just to themselves, their families, their employees, and their investors but also to other women hoping to follow in their footsteps. They feel that their personal failure plays into the stereotype of women being less capable as business owners. They worry that their failure reflects negatively on their entire gender.

- Of course, female founders don't fail more often than men. According to the 2022 Annual Report from the National Women's Business Council, women-owned firms grew 16.7 percent between 2012 and 2019 compared to the 5.2 percent growth rate for men-owned firms during the same period,[22] making them less likely to fail.

Still, as ALearn founder Kathryn Hanson points out,

People will fail. Almost everybody I know who has been on multiple start-ups has had some wins and some losses. You're in good company but at the end of the day, it is still challenging to be in a company when it fails.

No one plans to be part of the 70 percent of businesses that don't make it, and no one plans for some of the other "big falls" we'll see in this chapter. But part of an eyes-wide-open approach means that you need to work for the best but plan for the worst.

---

21 Josh Howarth, "Startup failure rate statistics (2023)," Exploding Topics, March 16, 2023, https://explodingtopics.com/blog/startup-failure-stats.

22 National Women's Business Council Annual Report, 2022, https://www.nwbc.gov/annual-reports/2022/.

Charting a Smooth Landing

Everyone has heard horror stories of employees waking up to a boilerplate email from HR telling them that they have to turn in their company computers by the end of the day and vacate the premises. The female trait of empathy can help founders to chart a better course. The entrepreneur in the opening story explained her process: "The second we decided we weren't going to keep going forward anymore, we needed to stop as quickly as possible and not continue to burn money."

She said,

> We put a lot of thought into how to do it. I worked with a business coach, talked to my investors, and even talked to other founders who had been through it. We were determined to find the best way to handle the situation.

She learned a lot from the process.

In-person is best, but it's not always possible

"We were a hybrid team, so the call had to be over Zoom so that everyone was told together."

Don't wing the live event

"I had a script of what I wanted to say. I was so nervous. But being prepared meant I got through it."

Plan for every step of the process

"I had a full communication plan of what we were going to send out each day and how we were going to communicate with each stakeholder."

Give yourself grace

"This was the hardest thing I'd ever done as a founder."

Don't rush yourself

"I don't think I could have rushed the process. But as soon as I knew it was what we needed to do, I was prepared to act."

After she made the announcement on a teary Zoom call, she reported,

> I had multiple people on the team reaching out to me, saying that they really appreciated how I handled it and also checking in on me. Getting that reaction gave me a lot of comfort. My team knew I cared about them and that I was doing everything I could.

FOUNDER KATHRYN HANSON ON TRANSITIONS:

I started a company called eMentoring back in the nineties before the internet was well established. I wasn't having luck raising money. This was in 1999—and the big crash came in 2000 for start-up companies. I merged eMentoring into another company, Pensare, where the CEO was also a woman. We were part of that big crash of 2000. That was not a fun time. It was really intense because we tried to hold on. And she tried to get Arthur Andersen to buy us. It almost worked but didn't at the end of the day. It was really tense, and the office was a horrible place to be because everybody was thinking they were going to lose their job. Companies were going under daily, and you knew that. It looked like we had a lifeline and then all of a sudden, it just crashed. It was tough emotionally for everybody. It's even tougher if you're in a room where everybody knows it's either now or never. And then all of a sudden, it's never, and everybody's cleaning out their desk. It's very deflating, de-energizing, a real mess. I'm still friends, actually, with several of the people I worked with on that company. A couple that worked for me in later ventures. So, you salvage what you can and sometimes it's a friendship.

Losing Control

Another way founders get hit with setbacks is when they start to lose control of what they worked so hard to build.

I had never planned to be in the CEO role for the long haul at Hitch. I had a two-year plan: by June 2022, I was going to step out of the CEO role so I could focus on GTM (go-to-market) efforts and bring in someone to handle the next series of funding rounds. My plan was that I would still act as the face of the company. I would be the primary draw for fundraising, evangelizing our product in the market, and acquiring customers. I would bring in a new and trusted COO now who could help with fundraising and take over as CEO in two years. It needed to be someone collaborative, someone I could trust with the care of "my baby." We needed to be aligned on the long-term vision, and I had to trust that relationship. I soon found this person, but at the last minute, he backed out.

In the summer of 2021, the board convinced me to bring in one of their own as COO and president. My lead investor and I had a very serious discussion around that. I asked him directly if it was his intention to take me out of the CEO role, and he told me that was not his plan. This was to give me more focus on customers versus operations and an experienced partner in fundraising.

My instincts were telling me that change was afoot. However, as was always my way, I accepted the situation with hope, a growth mindset, and a spirit of abundance. There was room for all. Also, this new COO was a woman, and elevating women was always one of my values. She had a lot of experience raising funds. I was hopeful for the future of Hitch and our ability to work together.

Unfortunately, from the very beginning, I felt that this wasn't going to be smooth sailing. Despite my being the CEO, the new governance model was that we would take it to the board if there was a disagreement between us. All major decisions on strategy, product, or key hires would be made together. I had been a talent architect most of my career. I knew from personal experience that, under these conditions, having two primary leaders could lead to friction.

Looking back, I see all the proactive things I could have done to right the situation. But hindsight is twenty-twenty. I tell this story now from a perspective of strength as someone who has lived and learned. I'm so much stronger now for having gone through it and having made mistakes that I'll never make again. As the saying goes, what doesn't kill you makes you stronger. And, as someone who tries to find the silver lining in all things—despite our struggles, it was because she and I found a way to work together that we had a good ending. In this case, I came out the other side not just a better founder but also a better leader and more experienced all-around business-woman, and I'm thankful for the experiences, even the painful ones.

But at the time, I wasn't sure what to do, so I did what Allison Baum Gates calls, "eating glass." In other words, I did whatever needed to be done with grit and fortitude. I put on a smile and pushed forward with everything I had. Hitch needed the funding, and my investors and the board wanted the change. The pressure to keep the company financially viable and moving forward was always my main priority. I was not going to disappoint all the people who believed in me—my board, my investors, my team, my family, and myself. Unfortunately, even with the addition of the new COO, we kept on pitching investors and customers, but we were still challenged to get the outcomes we aspired for.

Five months later, right before Thanksgiving, my investor came to my house for one of our typical one-on-one walks. It was still the time of social distancing because of the COVID-19 pandemic, so that was how we met. We got about halfway down the block from my house when he told me they were going to take me out as CEO and put the COO in my place.

My first reaction was shock. Despite that we were experiencing some challenges, I was still totally blindsided on not being asked to participate in such a major decision for my company. I asked a lot of questions about this. We walked probably for about twenty minutes. To be honest, I don't remember a lot of that conversation because of the range of emotions battling inside of me.

We said our goodbyes. I walked into my house, sat at my desk, and said to myself, *What the hell just happened? Oh my God, am I losing control of my company?* This was my worst fear. But I didn't have time to be afraid. My job now was to figure out what to do next.

Handling the Transition

I kept on working as hard for Hitch as ever, but I can't deny that I felt hollowed out. That whole week, I felt out-of-body. Meanwhile, life went on, and I needed the company to keep moving forward. We had to make sure everything was legally buttoned up, including what role I was to play moving forward. I was still a major shareholder in the company.

And yet, I was not seeing a clear path in front of me. I had tons of reservations. I knew I could immediately go back to a high-paying executive job if I wanted to, but this was my baby, and I was not a quitter. I had to see it through and check my ego at the door. After all, this was the section of the story that should have been familiar. I was warned of this potential outcome by other founders. Specifically, when venture investors get itchy, one of the ways they can take control back is to trade out the CEO for one of their own or other leadership transitions.

ANONYMOUS FOUNDER ON LOSING CONTROL:

I was facing a tricky business situation in which we had to move hundreds of customers from one platform to another. The natural outcome of this was a loss of customers. Board members and investors suddenly wanted to bring in another person to replace me. There was all at once this feeling of *she doesn't know what she's doing.* And I was out.

The new operational head was also a woman who now reported directly to the main investors. I realized after the fact that this was my fault. Legally, it didn't have to be this way. But because of my inexperience, I allowed the situation to unfold. Even though I still remained CEO, I was not an operational CEO, and our board was really a name-only board, and the business was de facto being run by this person who was pretty much a pawn of the investor.

So, the investor was trying to run the business from the backseat, and that did not go well. The investor was not operational and had never been operational. He didn't have that experience. But he felt comfortable weighing in, and he brought in somebody who had not had P&L experience. So, it was inexperience meets inexperience, set up to not collaborate or be accountable to the person who had total experience—me.

It was not a good phase for the company. It eventually got to a point where it was obvious there had to be a transition. The investor took a backseat and stopped trying to control the business from the sidelines. But it had to get to a pretty obvious space for that to happen. It was a lost opportunity. We could have really grown and done some pretty exciting things in that time, but we didn't. If he had a little bit of faith that the woman entrepreneur who saw the market opportunity, saw what the market needed, built a product to respond to the market needs, and knew the customer inside and out things may have gone differently.

Like me, despite the struggles, this founder didn't want to quit on her company. It had been her whole career, so there was no question that she would stick it out. She said, "I was a trooper for a year, but it was not fun at all. It was pretty toxic." She learned lessons that mirrored my own. She advised:

ACT EARLY

I was in reactive mode. It was half a year of not great, and then leading up to a year of really not great. I wish I'd sat down in the earliest phases and said, "Okay, so here's how I'm analyzing the situation. In order to give you confidence that this is going to be a good return for you, let me tell you how I see the business, my role in the business, my capability of taking the business from where we are now to a better outcome."

CALL OUT THE SITUATION

I let the situation get toxic. That was my inexperience. As humans, we're a little slow on the uptake, so it's not until after we're done that our brain catches up and processes. I really should have managed it proactively.

I couldn't agree more.

Eyes Wide Open

If I played the reels backward to when my lead investor came in, he had voiced concerns from the start about the fact that I hadn't been a CEO before. He had told me in so many words that I was a bit of a calculated risk because of my background. He even told me stories about how he'd transitioned founders and CEOs to other roles before with great success. In a sense, he had previewed what might be his long-term plan.

But you hear what you want to hear.

When I look back, maybe I was a little too confident about my ability to overcome his preconceptions. He was pointing out truths—I hadn't been a CEO before. However, that is a core theme in my life. Every job I took on that I may not have had the qualifications or experience for on paper, I not only rose to the occasion but over-achieved across the board, which landed me into the next big thing. I had a lot of confidence in my ability to learn and grow and always knew how to put people around me who might be better or smarter than me in some key areas to make up for any of my gaps.

I have thought long and hard about whether being a woman had anything to do with some of my experiences and those of other female founders who have told me similar stories. I can't really say for sure. But one thing I do know is that as we move away from the stereotypes of who can be successful founders and CEOs and who can't, the type of background that I had and others like me will be more appreciated. All of the skills and experiences that many of us have acquired over the course of our personal and professional lives won't be discounted in the same way. In the future, I truly believe that people will be forced to get better at connecting the dots between what exists and what is possible.

Allison Baum Gates explains,

We have to shine a light on internal bias. I highlight the woman's track record. Focus on the positives of the kind of operational excellence she has achieved. Maybe she wasn't necessarily a CEO previously, but she was a chief product officer or a chief marketing officer, and these are the things that she was able to accomplish in that role. She grew revenue from X, Y, Z. I think that it's easy to sit around and be bitter when people react with bias and shut down and choose not to engage, but for me, the only way that we can educate people and get them over the line is to make sure that we're prepared for those questions, we recognize that that's the reality and that we have numbers and facts and figures in our back pocket to be able to answer those questions and say, "Hey. Maybe her resume doesn't look exactly like some of our male CEOs but here's what she has done and here's why it's relevant."

A good example of this already happening is around the debate over whether a CHRO belongs on a board. Most boards are made of CFOs and CEOs. CHRO is a very different discipline. I highlight my unique experience around the acquisition of talent, which is a huge risk for a company and important for a board to have oversight. Also, a CHRO understands compensation and can add that expertise to the board. There are also issues with succession, both for the CEO and other executives. The CHRO can play a critical leadership role in guiding that process.

So how do you develop another set of leaders? Well, CHROs know that very well. What happens when the company goes through a M&A integration of two companies? That's about the people primarily and understanding how to get the best contribution from whatever you've acquired. The role of the CHRO on boards is already growing, but it's not there yet. So, we're all in the position of having to sell ourselves. We have to connect the dots for people in order to show them the value of our unique contributions. They won't just automatically see it. They're trained to look for financial acumen. They're trained to look for what they've seen in the past. You can call that bias. You can call that human nature. Or, you can call it out and be a part of making change happen, not just for yourself but also for all the people coming behind you.

Women Need to Support One Another

Although it is exciting to see the momentum shifting with the emergence of more female funds and VCs, not everyone has had positive experiences. One female founder shared,

> The irony of my situation was that some of the women who invested in me weren't there when I needed them most. They said the right things: "we'll support you" and "we'll help you" and "we'll work through this"—and then they did the opposite.

This founder wasn't alone in seeing this behavior from female investors who were supposed to do better. She explained that they didn't live by their credos and that this is what ultimately makes things worse for all of us. The general consensus among these women was that something had to be done about this—that this type of behavior was going to set us back decades.

The thing I decided to do is call it out here, on paper: the biggest risk for female founders is female investors putting on a guise of solidarity when their actions don't align to the mission they espouse.

Another founder told me,

> I was totally off my game because I just assumed because they are women, they're not going to screw me. Their whole mission was around helping women, and so I was off my game in terms of my own due diligence about who they were and what they stood for.

Deidre Paknad, CEO and co-founder of WorkBoard, has seen this kind of behavior. She says,

I think sometimes women had to work too hard to get their seat at the table. That created a gap between why they wanted to be at the table for themselves and why they wanted to be there for the greater good. Once in the chair, they faced a dilemma. They didn't want anyone to think they had an agenda, "a woman thing," even when they did believe in the "woman thing" and even when they were hired because the fund wanted to look like *they* had a "woman thing."

Paknad believes that things are changing, and I hope she's right. She explains,

In 2018, 2019, we were all trying to figure out what it meant to be at the table, trying to get enough guts to represent and not feel like we had to apologize. I think that made for a messy few years.

Paknad advises the answer is, as always, to lean into your strengths and learn from your mistakes. She says that in her first company, she actually believed a founding CEO *should* be replaced, because that was what was often done, and so she willingly stepped aside. But at her second company, she "learned I could have just believed in myself. I didn't know that before, so I chickened out on whether I had what it took. I listened too much to external talk."

Women Raising Up Other Women

The flip side of women not supporting one another is that there are women who genuinely make an effort to uplift and support other women. I was so fortunate to have many of those amazing female investors, mentors, and advocates, such as Judy O'Brien who guided me along my journey through some of the most painful moments and key decision points of my career. The good news is there are too many of them to give proper credit in these pages, but my gratitude runs deep, and I did my best in the Acknowledgments of this book to call out some of these "sHEROEs" because we need more of them.

It turned out that three great female leaders in technology were the ones who saw the value of our solution and our people; namely, the fact that it was female-founded, female-funded, and female-led. They did everything in their power to ensure our success as we moved through the prospective acquisition conversations with one of the most successful platform companies in the world.

These women were Melanie Lougee, Gretchen Alarcon, and Amanda Vinson. They did the sourcing, evaluation, and advocacy to turn Hitch from an early-stage start-up on the rise to my dream of being a ubiquitous technology play that could change the world.

This is all to say that I had a community of amazing women, and when I reached out, it rallied to my side. That I didn't in the moment reach out enough was one of my biggest regrets. Keeping our most painful stories to ourselves is supposed to be a sign of strength, but when we tell them, we find out that we're not alone, and that makes us all stronger in the end.

Lessons from Female Founders on Managing the Pivots and Transitions

Doing a start-up is not a logical thing. You have to be passionate about what you're doing because the chances of success are not that high, whether you're in for-profit or nonprofit, I've seen both go under. And you have to absolutely believe that you can make a difference and be willing to push through the hard times. That passion and resilience are both requirements for a CEO, and maybe a little bit of cockiness or at least self-confidence that allows you to really say, "We can do this." In for-profit and nonprofit, I had real faith that we would be able to make it through. And you have to believe that because a lot of people are going to tell you no … and you've got to be able to be okay with that and move on.

—KATHRYN HANSON, CEO AND FOUNDER, ALEARN

There are two different mindsets as a founder. One, you need to just hang on no matter what and fight through everything and against all odds and stick it out, versus the fail-fast mindset. For me, the two were like an angel and devil on my shoulders. Who do you listen to? Ultimately, I didn't want my ego to be part of this decision. We looked at the facts and decided.

—ANONYMOUS FOUNDER

I feel like my entrepreneurial journey is not over. I'm already looking to the next thing. There's so much I could take away from all these experiences. My self-worth is not tied up in it. This is the odds with start-ups, and I don't regret anything along the whole journey.

—ANONYMOUS FOUNDER

Chapter 10

THE EXIT-FOR FOUNDERS AND COMPANIES

NAVIGATING THE END GAME AND SUSTAINING YOUR VISION

> *As a founder, sometimes your strength is about seeing your exit strategy clearly when others might not.*
>
> **—KELLEY STEVEN-WAISS**

By early 2022, I was starting to see how we had successfully created a market, but no good idea goes unpunished. That also meant more competition and the realization that we needed to have the funding to scale our solution to serve the enterprise. From the board's perspective, we had some disagreements about the timing of our exit strategy. But in my mind, there were two ways forward to see our vision through: exit to a larger strategic or to raise a Series A.

"Exiting to a Strategic" means being acquired by a larger company because your technology is integral to their core strategy. Typically, when you are acquired, the acquiring company is evaluating your ARR (annual recurring revenue). They're acquiring your customers and the value of your company: the cash you have on hand plus the revenue that's going to come in current and future contracts. Your sales pipeline becomes a window into that promising future. But there is also the option that a company might acquire your start-up and pursue more of a strategic valuation because of interest in your technology.

Because of the consolidation in the market and the fact that we were still at such an early stage compared to our competitors, I felt we should be acquired by a strategic where our vision could be fully realized. Our closest competitors were on C and D rounds and well ahead of us in terms of scaling their operations. Although Hitch had become a darling in the market with a brand bigger than we were, we still had competitors with even more traction in the market and a lot more signed customers. Despite the recent leadership transition, not much had changed, so these two scenarios needed to be vetted. Yet, the consensus with the majority of the board was to still pursue a Series A.

We were getting knocks on the door—interest from potential buyers. Most founders don't ever want to let go. They want to hang on and ignore offers from the outside. But given what I could see around the corner and the current market, I felt we should answer the call. Part of the responsibility of being a CEO is to understand when there's an opportunity for shareholders to make money, an opportunity to have a major win. I wasn't the acting CEO anymore, but I still felt that responsibility. It was so important to me that I found a way for *everyone* to win.

Two major suitors approached us, but after a few meetings, the decision was made by our board not to engage. They believed that Hitch would not get the valuation it deserved, so we continued to look for that big Series A and continued investing in the long haul.

From my standpoint, if we were to entertain an exit via acquisition, we needed a company where our technology could be scaled in order to realize our vision of making work better for everyone. What I started to see was an opportunity to become part of something much bigger where the GTM (go-to-market) engine was more mature, and our technology would have a chance to be ubiquitous. I knew that we had more power with inbounds. I also knew that where there was one, there would be many.

And then we got *the* call—the one you dream about. At least, it was the one I certainly dreamed about. ServiceNow arrived at our door at the end of February 2022. ServiceNow is a platform company that helps digitize and unify organizations. They're strategically placed at the experience layer on top of a lot of legacy systems. Its single, unified platform integrates seamlessly with different systems. I saw the potential for Hitch's skills intelligence technology to be ubiquitous. By re-platforming Hitch's skills intelligence software into their platform, we would not only be able to serve HR use cases in the future but also potentially enable all work flexibility on the basis of skills. It could put Hitch on a platform where there are thousands of customers.

My objective was always to change the world and make it better for people. There was no better suitor than ServiceNow to make this dream a reality. Service-Now was a rocket ship with a dynamic and charismatic chairman and CEO, Bill McDermott. ServiceNow was well-regarded and had more than doubled in size during the pandemic. As Sheryl Sandberg puts it, "If you're offered a seat on a rocket ship, don't ask what seat. Just get on."

> "If you're offered a seat on a rocket ship, don't ask what seat. Just get on."

The decision was made to engage, and the Hitch board was finally all on the same page. We locked arms as a leadership team because it was clear that this potential exit was best for everyone.

Quiet Moments and Reflections

I loved Hitch and believed in the dream it stood for. Despite any turmoil that might have been going on through the transition, it paid off to check my ego at the door and remember why I started Hitch. I was obsessed with my mission and told myself this was a moment of validation and opportunity. But still, it wasn't easy.

Despite all this good news, the transitions of the last several months were starting to catch up with me. I was elated—as well as exhausted. I was so close to the finish line, but that last mile is always the hardest, even if it's downhill. My lead investor was starting to pick up on the taxing nature of the last several months and took me out for a coffee in Palo Alto. He told me that he knew these recent changes were hard for me, and he offered that I do some things that give me energy and mental focus. Talking to him over coffee reminded me of the importance of maintaining my mental health, keeping perspective, and also reminded me that I had another, stronger power: the power to persevere.

My mother had always taught me to persevere. When I was young and I may have wanted to quit dance or softball or some other activity I was in because of a challenge I was facing, my mother taught me that there were going to be times when it was hard or uncomfortable. The instinct is to quit or walk away, but that is when you need to dig in. The same is true in marriage or when kids get difficult. But it's your beloved, your kid, your company, your dream of a better world for potentially millions of people. I had survived so many situations in my personal and professional lives. I had gone through difficult relationships with bullies and bad actors. I had survived my mother's passing in a very tragic way. A reel of positive affirmations began with that little voice from my mother. I told myself: *just put your feet on the ground and keep moving forward. You can make it through whatever comes your way. You've done it before.*

Taking the Win

When Hitch became part of ServiceNow, I was not only exhausted in some ways but also exhilarated. My people landed in great roles in a great company. My investors all got an outstanding return on their investment. Now we had the infrastructure and scale to propel us four to five years forward. When I look back and ask myself if Hitch was successful or not, the answer is absolutely yes, 100 percent. This was a huge success on all levels. And yet for a founder, it can be a similar feeling to achieving a huge milestone and realizing you suddenly don't have that mission you woke up every day fighting for. You are now asking yourself, *what's next?* You may feel a little bit lost. However, be kind to yourself. You're now opening a new chapter.

It's also important to note that you don't have to have a big exit to be a success. There are several ways an exit can happen, and along with your personal interests, you must establish the outcome that best serves all investors. To find this, you need to ask where the maximum value exists. The value can look like

- staying the course and continuing to fundraise or take new investors (angels, large funds, or venture) or even continuing to fund operations with existing revenue or bootstrapping it yourself;

- a partnership with another company;

- being acquired or sold;

- an IPO (initial public offering); or

- an alternative structure, such as an employee buyout

All these options have positives and negatives. If you've not exited a company before or taken one public, reach out to your personal board of directors and get a lesson on what to watch out for. Remember that you're looking out for yourself, your shareholders, your employees, and your dream. How can your mission and purpose be best realized?

Even if what happens in the end isn't the story you've been telling yourself and it didn't come out the way you would have written it, your success might be that you learned something about yourself. Or maybe it taught you something about a market that will lead you to the next big thing. There are a hundred things that can happen that were unscripted but result in one kind of success or another. It's your job to find the silver lining, to allow yourself to celebrate what you learned, to really focus on that, and to move forward to your next big thing.

Much later, after the deal was done and I had joined ServiceNow, I ran into Bill McDermott, the chairman and CEO of ServiceNow, in the hallway on the executive floor of our headquarters in Santa Clara. I decided, *this is my moment. I'm going to introduce myself.* I stopped him, boldly put out my hand, and said,

> I'm Kelley Steven-Waiss, the founder of Hitch. I have to tell you, when Hitch was acquired, it was a dream come true because I truly believe that the best way we could change the world was by joining forces with a platform like ServiceNow.

Of course, he loved hearing that. But it was the truth. My truth. And in the end, I'm so glad that I saw the process through, and we had the opportunity to take that vision to reality.

Integrating into a New Company

It can be a really strange feeling when you get acquired and suddenly you have a new identity. You are no longer leading the small start-up, and your team may need to adjust to new roles, new processes, and new leaders. Be sure to take some time to mentally transition from one to the other. Take the time to celebrate what you and the team have accomplished and be there to support one another on the challenges in integrating into the new organization.

We had a huge virtual celebration with our team and spent time on affirmations about each person's role in the success of Hitch. It was a great opportunity to show appreciation for the many contributions that led to the success. As a founder, it was a very proud moment for me. I had several people (too many to name) who had been on the journey with me and some who had been with me from the very start—Weibke Hurrelmann, Thomas Bielagk, Nick McClure, and Rainer Oviir. I remember feeling incredibly grateful (and still am) for their loyalty and commitment to the roller-coaster ride they had been on and how much each of them had contributed along the way.

The Founder's Exit: When and How to Exit as the Founder

Aside from the company's exit that might look like an IPO, being acquired, or handing over to employees, there's the issue of the individual founder exiting. At some point, every founder must define success for themselves and their investors. There's often a time to leave a company behind to move on to other things. It's a balance of risk and reward.

In 2001, when Barbara Fagan founded ROI Communications, a company specializing in internal communications, she knew she wanted an exit strategy at some point. She was thinking of five years. But then, as she puts it, "the business takes on a life of its own. It kept me engaged because we were growing and there were always new things to figure out."

In 2015, she had a lot of interest in buyouts from several sources. She says, "It all sounded very alluring, exciting, and flattering." She hired an investment banker to put the company up for sale and started having management meetings."

Meanwhile, she was talking to other founders who had sold their companies. She says,

> They were telling me stories of how their companies had gotten destroyed, especially the culture. Sometimes selling is

the right thing for people to do, but I saw that I just couldn't do it. No amount of money would be worth watching what I'd worked so hard to build be destroyed.

That was when she learned about ESOPs (Employee Stock Ownership Plans). The employees don't buy the company. They get a benefit. Fagan says,

> It's like a pension plan. It's complicated, but basically, it's an alternative way for the company to buy the founder out through loans which give employees the benefit of the growth of the company. You have to have a healthy company that's profitable to make it work because you have to take out a loan, and then over time, the owners get bought out. I've been partially bought out, and the rest will come in the years to come. But it has made such a wonderful difference in the company. We started to grow faster immediately. The employees are so engaged. And I get to move on to other things knowing my company is in good hands.

If you're considering a personal exit from your company, ask yourself:

- *Am I still enjoying it, or is my mental health or my wellness suffering overall?*

- *Am I sacrificing things that I value?*

- *Am I still effective as the leader of this company?*

If the answer to any of these questions is *no*, then it might be time for your exit. It's hard to face that maybe when it's time for the company to scale, the person to do that isn't you. Those are very hard decisions for founders to make. Founders don't always take the company ten, twenty, or even thirty years out. Sometimes, you need new blood, new thinking.

Think about your situation carefully. Once you hand over the leadership baton, you don't have the same level of authority or influence you had before. However, it still can be a good outcome for you and your company.

When Barbara Fagan began to transition her company to her employees, she says, "Before, I had total power, frankly. It was my business. I could do what I wanted with it. I could take money out of it for whatever I wanted. And now it's much more of an egalitarian system."

However, she says,

I really knew it was time. My heart and my soul said, *you can't be spending this much time thinking about these things anymore*. It was time to be contributing to the world in a different way and even contributing to ROI in a different way. This was the right path for me. I will continue to be a part of ROI. I'll be the founder, and our culture will remain intact. I'll never completely go away.

LESSONS FROM FEMALE FOUNDERS
The Exit

One of the most circular arguments still happening today is that there are too few big exits of female founders. However, when you look at the numbers, since we under-invested in women, there is a smaller pool of female-founded businesses to begin with. A small sample size does increase the difficulty. We need larger numbers of female-founded businesses so people can see the track record they expect. There are still a lot of gender stereotypes that lead to this type of bias.

—MIRIAM RIVERA, CEO, CO-FOUNDER, AND
MANAGING DIRECTOR, ULU VENTURES

I evaluate everything as an opportunity cost. What else could I have been doing with my time? And it helps me value if what I'm doing is worthwhile, because I think to myself, "How has that time helped move my mission forward, or helped me personally in some way?" And this topic is a lifelong topic for me. It guides me to when I should pursue something, or when it's time to move on.

—DENISE BROUDER, FOUNDER, SWAY

When and how to exit is driven by external factors. If the IPO window is open, there's only one right answer—you're going public. If the IPO window is closed—you're getting acquired. You don't get to call whether the window is open or closed when your company is at the right level of maturity. You just don't know. You don't control it.

—DEIDRE PAKNAD, CEO AND CO-FOUNDER, WORKBOARD

I am a serial founder, so I've had two exits. I've seen it all … and in the end I will be known to some extent as a professional who achieved great things financially, who was innovative and motivating and hard driving. But at the end of the day, we all need to really think about what we want our legacy to be. It is easier to get up in the morning and easier to go to sleep at night if we have as part of that mission or part of that legacy to make the world a little bit better than the way we came into it.

—SHEILA TALTON, CEO AND FOUNDER,
GRAY MATTER ANALYTICS

Conclusion

Interviewing so many amazing women for this book was such an honor, but it also raised a question in the back of my mind as I wrote: *what if the problem of bias against female founders had passed?* Each female founder's story illustrated so much hope and positivity, especially the stories from younger founders, that I started to doubt whether this movement was even still needed. Maybe, just maybe, this problem of bias toward female founders was behind us. *Was I writing about a problem of my generation, which no longer applied to the next?*

I began writing and interviewing in early 2023. By the end of January, the proceeding year's data finally was compiled: all-female teams got 1.9 percent of total US venture capital, *down from the year before.*

While it was clearly possible for individual women to succeed, and I'm proud to have told those stories in this book, the overall numbers are still not trending up. The good news is that in our discussions about the issues we faced as female founders, we found there are solutions and ways around the bias that still plagues us.

I can only hope that in the not-too-distant future, this book becomes irrelevant as the tides of bias will have passed. But for now, the need for an eyes-wide-open approach is still necessary.

I want to leave you with four key insights I learned from my experience and from speaking with so many female founders that I believe will make a difference.

INSIGHT #1:
Invest in Female Founders

We need to put our money where our mouths are. We need to take smart risks and invest in other women. The only way that happens is when more women get into venture to put money behind other women's great ideas, supporting them, making introductions, and not making the bar too high. The "good old boy's club" needs to be matched with the power of the new girl's club. We need to pledge that those of us in a financial position to give back will do so with our money, our advice, our contacts, and anything else we have to change the data before our granddaughters are seeking funding. It is my intention to practice what I preach, and I urge others inspired by the stories in this book to do the same.

INSIGHT #2:
Raise Up Other Women

Nothing that I heard in the stories women told me for this book and nothing that I experienced in my own career makes me more sad than when women proclaim values that they don't live. It takes us one step forward and two steps back. Many women interviewed for this book, and many others I know took investment from venture funds that espoused to support women, and they got burned. Some didn't want their names used, as they were still in the throes of trying to finance their businesses. Do your due diligence. A woman who espouses to support other women and then doesn't is more dangerous than a man who tells it like it is. We have to find more ways to lift one another up and move away from competition to a spirit of mutual collaboration.

INSIGHT #3:
Innovate and Make a Difference

The world moves forward when the best ideas make it to fruition no matter who presents them. Believe in yourself, and lean into the differences that will propel you forward. No matter how much the world tells you that you can't take on the role, in the end, only you can keep yourself in the game, so don't knock yourself before you get started. Don't listen to the voices saying you can't do it. Despite the odds, it's critical that we continue to look for ways to improve people's lives. If you have the passion to solve some of the world's biggest problems, you need to stay the course. You just might change the world in a profound way, and you will send a positive message to those women who come behind you.

INSIGHT #4:
Be the Change You Wish to See

We're not going to change anything if we keep on doing things the same way they've always been done. Women have superpowers like empathy, collaboration, consensus-building, and a deep sense of purpose, which are hallmarks of successful female founders. There is something fundamentally different about how successful women operate in the business world. We need to lean into that and make sure we continue encouraging more women to bring their ideas forward, and even more importantly, that we look for opportunities to support each other along the way.

I truly believe that, together, we can change the landscape for female founders. I hope that this book in some way helps move us toward that goal. We all need to work together to try to make the world a better, more productive place for *everyone*.

—Kelley Steven-Waiss